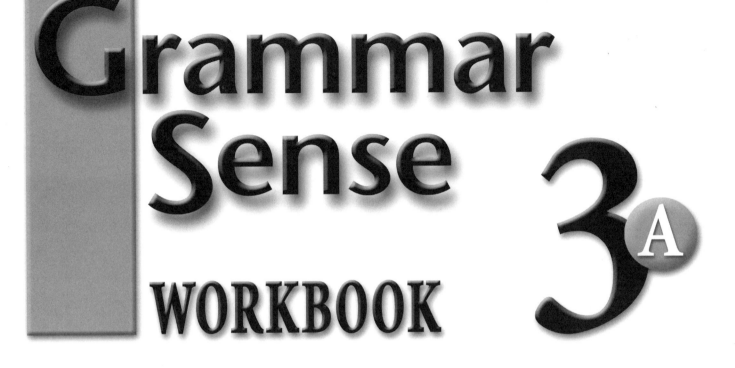

Grammar Sense 3A
WORKBOOK

Angela Blackwell and Karen Davy

OXFORD

UNIVERSITY PRESS

OXFORD
UNIVERSITY PRESS

198 Madison Avenue
New York, NY 10016 USA

Great Clarendon Street
Oxford OX2 6DP England

Oxford   New York
Auckland   Bangkok   Buenos Aires   Cape Town   Chennai
Dar es Salaam   Delhi   Hong Kong   Istanbul   Karachi   Kolkata
Kuala Lumpur   Madrid   Melbourne   Mexico City   Mumbai
Nairobi   São Paulo   Shanghai   Taipei   Tokyo   Toronto

OXFORD is a trademark of Oxford University Press.

ISBN 0-19-436627-8

Copyright © 2004 Oxford University Press

Editorial Manager: Janet Aitchison
Editorial Development, Project Management,
  and Production: Marblehead House, Inc.
Production Manager: Shanta Persaud
Production Coordinator: Zainaltu Jawat Ali

Illustrations: Roger Penwill
Cover Design: Lee Ann Dollison
Cover Photo: Kevin Schafer / Peter Arnold, Inc.

The authors and publisher are grateful for permission to reprint the following photographs:

p. 7 ©Jon Feingersh / CORBIS; **p. 8** ©The Dian Fossey Gorilla Fund International (www.gorillafund.org); **p. 13** ©Jack Hollingsworth / Photodisc ; **p. 22** ©Charlotte Casey; **p. 29** ©AFP / CORBIS; **p. 34** ©CORBIS; **p. 59** ©Dennis Degnan / CORBIS

Printing (last digit): 10 9 8 7 6 5 4 3 2 1

Printed in Hong Kong

Contents

Chapter **1 The Present** 1

Chapter **2 The Past** 8

Chapter **3 Future Forms** 15

    Review: Chapters 1–3 20

Chapter **4 The Present Perfect** 22

Chapter **5 The Present Perfect Continuous** 29

Chapter **6 The Past Perfect and the Past Perfect Continuous** 36

    Review: Chapters 4–6 43

Chapter **7 Modals of Possibility** 46

Chapter **8 Past Modals** 53

    Review: Chapters 7–8 60

Answer Key 63

Key To Chapter Reviews 71

1 The Present

FORM

1 Examining Form

Read this newspaper article and complete the tasks below.

In Japan, *Kyoiku Mamas* Help Kids Succeed in School

TOKYO, Japan—Eleven-year-old Fumie is always tired. She is in the fifth grade. Three days a week, she rushes home from school, eats a
5 quick snack, and then runs out again on her way to *juku*, or cram school. She's preparing to enter a good private school next year.

Her three-and-a-half-year-old
10 brother, Koichi, goes to nursery school. He's getting ready to take one of the most important examinations of his life—entrance into the first grade.
15 These children are likely to do well because their mother knows what it takes to succeed in today's highly competitive Japan. She's called a *kyoiku mama*, or "education
20 mother." The education mother studies with her children, takes them to special classes, and hires tutors for them. She never leaves them in the hands of a babysitter
25 even if she does sometimes want to have an afternoon for herself. She knows that her children's time is too important for that. In contrast, Japanese fathers don't get as
30 involved in their children's education. They usually work very late and come home long after their families are already in bed.

Today more Japanese are
35 becoming aware of the harmful effects of too much studying. They realize that their children are spending too much time with their books, playing too little, and
40 possibly sleeping too little. But until the system changes, the *kyoiku mama* is unlikely to go away.

---

1. There are many examples of the simple present in the article. The first one is underlined. Underline eight more. (Don't include forms of *be*.)

2. There are six examples of the present continuous. The first one is circled. Circle five more.

3. Find the sentence in the simple present that includes *does* and draw a box around it. Why did the writer use *does*? Check the correct answer.

   _____ **a.** The sentence is a question.

   _____ **b.** The sentence is a statement that uses *does* for emphasis.

Read the answers below. Use the information in parentheses to write a simple present question for each answer.

1. (Koichi/go/to elementary school)

    Q: Does Koichi go to elementary school?

    A: No, he doesn't. He goes to nursery school.

2. (his sister Fumie/study/in sixth grade)

    Q: Does her sister Fumie study in sixth grade?

    A: No she doesn't. She studies in fifth grade.

3. (how many days/she/go/to juku)

    Q: How many days does she go to juku?

    A: Three days a week.

4. (their mother/study/with her children)

    Q: Does their mother study with her children?

    A: Yes, she does.

5. (she/teach them/herself)

    Q: Does she teach them herself?

    A: No, she doesn't. She hires tutors.

6. (why/Japanese fathers/not get involved/in their children's education)

    Q: Why don't Japanese fathers not get involved in their children's education?

    A: Because they usually work very late.

7. (when/they/usually/come/home)

    Q: When do they usually come home?

    A: Long after their families are in bed asleep.

8. (what/more Japanese/realize/today)

    Q: What do more Japanese realize today?

    A: Their children study too much and play too little.

Complete this paragraph with the present continuous form of the verbs in parentheses. Use contractions when possible.

Reporter: This is Chris Meeks in Wimbledon, England, next to the courts on

the first day of the tennis tournament. Right now the sun _is shining_ (shine),
                                                            1

and the seats _are filling up_ (fill up) quickly. Today, here on center court, we
              2

are looking (look) forward to watching a thrilling opening match. Here come
 3

the players. They_'re walking_ (walk) onto the court. What _is_ the American,
              4

Michael Powell, _doing_ (do)? _Is_ he _arguing_ (argue) with
                5   6

the Australian, Tim Chang? No, I'm sorry. He _isn't arguing_ (not/argue) with him.
                                            7

I think he_'s_ just _wishing_ (wish) him good luck. Well, the players
                    8

are taking off (take off) their warm-up suits and the game _is_ finally
 9

getting started (get started). Powell_'s taking_ (take) a last drink of water,
 10   11

and Chang _is doing_ (do) the same. The crowd _is making_ (make) a lot
          12   13

of noise, and the officials _are raising_ (raise) their hands to ask them to quiet
                            14

down. Here we go. Chang _is starting_ (start) his serve . . .
                        15

MEANING AND USE

4 · Contrasting the Simple Present and the Present Continuous

Read this conversation and complete the tasks below.

Ana: Hey, Carlos. How are you doing? How are things?

Carlos: Good. I'm back at college. I'm working on a degree in biology at Rutgers. It's a lot of work, but I love it.

Ana: Fantastic! That's a great school. And are you living near campus?

Carlos: I'm living at home with my parents—just for this semester.

Ana: How are you getting along with them?

Carlos: We get along OK, except they're always asking me where I'm going and when I'm coming home.

Ana: Well, you know what they say: "To your parents, you never grow up. You're always their child."

Carlos: Yeah, I guess that's right. But most of the time, things are fine. Especially because we hardly see each other. I leave for school every morning at 7:00 and don't get home until 11:00 at night.

Ana: So, will you be taking classes this summer?

Carlos: I don't think so. Every summer I work at my uncle's restaurant to help my family.

1. Read these sentences from the conversation. Write *SP* if they are in the simple present, and *PC* if they are in the present continuous.

   _PC_ **1.** I'm working on a degree in biology at Rutgers.

   _PC_ **2.** I'm living at home with my parents—just for this semester.

   _PC_ **3.** . . . except they're always asking me where I'm going and when I'm coming home.

   _SP_ **4.** "To your parents, you never grow up. You're always their child."

   _SP_ **5.** I leave for school every morning at 7:00, and I don't get home until 11:00 at night.

   _SP_ **6.** Every summer I work at my uncle's restaurant to help my family.

2. Now match each sentence to its use below.

   _5_ **a.** describing a routine

   _1_ **b.** expressing an activity in the extended present

   _6_ **c.** describing a habitual situation

   _3_ **d.** making a complaint

   _4_ **e.** describing a general truth

   _2_ **f.** describing a temporary situation

5 Understanding Verbs with Stative and Active Meanings

Read the sentences below. Write *S* for sentences that express states or conditions. Write *A* for sentences that express actions.

_S_ **1.** I own a bicycle.

_A_ **2.** I ride my bicycle after work.

_S_ **3.** I love riding my bicycle.

_A_ **4.** I also work out at a gym.

✗ _A_ **5.** I usually lift weights at the gym.

_S_ **6.** I believe that exercise is important.

_S_ **7.** I don't understand lazy people.

_S_ **8.** I feel good after exercising. S

COMBINING FORM, MEANING, AND USE

6 Thinking About Meaning and Use

Choose the correct response to each statement or question. There may be more than one correct answer for each.

1. "I'm living in a small apartment on Center Street."

The speaker . . .

a. is complaining

b. thinks her living situation is temporary

c. is describing an action in progress

d. wants to stay where she is

2. "What does Yuko do?"

The speaker wants to know . . .

a. Yuko's daily schedule

b. Yuko's occupation

c. a general truth about Yuko

d. the way Yuko feels

3. "I don't sleep more than four or five hours a night."

The speaker is talking about a . . .

a. routine

b. physical sensation

c. general truth

d. definition

4. "I really love this computer game."

   The speaker is . . .
   a. not playing the game
   b. expressing an emotion
   c. describing a typical quality
   d. expressing a physical sensation

5. "Fewer and fewer planes are flying to Italy this summer."

   The speaker is describing a . . .
   a. routine
   b. permanent situation
   c. changing situation
   d. habitual situation

6. "How often do you go to the doctor?"

   The speaker is asking about . . .
   a. an action in progress
   b. a general truth
   c. a person's routine
   d. a changing situation

7. "Beef contains more fat than poultry or fish."

   The speaker is talking about . . .
   a. a physical sensation
   b. a general truth
   c. a changing situation
   d. an emotion

8. "Police are questioning more than a dozen people about the crime."

   The speaker is describing . . .
   a. an action in progress
   b. a habitual situation
   c. a typical quality
   d. a changing situation

There are eleven errors in this magazine advice column. The first one has been corrected. Find and correct ten more.

Ask Dr. Frank

Dear Dr. Frank:

I ~~write~~ 'm writing this letter because I have a serious problem. I work in a stressful job, but I'm ~~not believing~~ don't believe it's worse than what most people face at work. My problem is that I'm ~~crying~~ cry too easily when things go~~s~~ wrong. I knowing I have to get stronger. I don't deal well with disappointment or criticism. It's ~~being~~ very embarrassing. In fact, the situation ~~becomes~~ is becoming more and more difficult. What advice do you have for me?

Cry Baby in Dallas

Dear Cry Baby:

Most of us get~~s~~ upset when others criticize us. But you are ~~being~~ right: You're ~~not appearing~~ don't appear professional when you cry at work. Sometimes we need~~s~~ to cry, but tears don't belong~~s~~ on the job. If you think you're going to cry, go to the restroom and do it there. And please, see a therapist to help you with your emotions.

Arlene Frank, M.D.

Follow the steps below to write a descriptive paragraph.

1. Find a photograph or drawing that shows a lot of activity. Study the picture carefully. What activities are happening? List some of the activities that you see. Then write notes describing people or objects in the picture.

2. On a separate sheet of paper, use your notes to write a detailed paragraph describing your picture. Use the present continuous to tell what is happening in the picture. Use the simple present to describe the people and objects.

> Here's a picture of my family at a picnic. My father is getting the fire ready for the barbecue. He's the large man in shorts . . . .

2 The Past

FORM

1 Examining Form

Read this short biography and complete the tasks below.

The Lonely Woman of the Forest

Dian Fossey and friend

American zoologist Dian Fossey first (became) interested in Africa in the early 1960s. She traveled there in 1963 and met the famous anthropologist Louis Leakey. Once, while Fossey and Leakey were talking 5 about mountain gorillas, she expressed her wish to study these animals' behavior. Four years later, she returned to Africa with a research grant from the National Geographic Society.

The mountain gorilla was becoming extinct when Fossey began her research. 10 Soon, she was at war with poachers who were killing gorillas in Rwanda's Parc National des Volcans. She also opposed Rwandan authorities, who hoped to open the park to tourism. In fact, she threatened to shoot any tourist who approached her station.

This dedication to her gorilla friends earned her enemies. One night in 1985, 15 Fossey was killed while she was sleeping at her campsite in the mountains of Rwanda.

Fossey's work made her a legend. At one time, there were only ten gorilla families still alive. Today, that number has more than doubled–thanks to "the lonely woman of the forest."

---

becoming extinct: dying out   **poacher:** a person who kills animals illegally

grant: money that is awarded for a specific purpose

1. There are many examples of the simple past in the biography. The first one is circled. Circle eight more. (Don't include forms of *be.*)

2. There are four examples of the past continuous. The first one is underlined. Underline three more.

3. There are three examples of time clauses beginning with *while* and *when.* One has a box around it. Find two more.

Use the cues to write conversations. Write *Conversation 1* in the simple past and *Conversation 2* in the past continuous.

Conversation 1

Rosa: why/be/you/late again this morning?

   <u>Why were you late again this morning?</u>

Hector: I/oversleep. I/not/wake up/until 8:30.

_____

Rosa: your boss/see/you?

_____

Hector: she/see/me/when/I/come/in.

_____

Rosa: she/say/anything to you?

_____

Hector: she/not/say/anything, but she/give/me a dirty look.

_____

Conversation 2

Elena: you and Sasha/make/a lot of noise last night.

   <u>You and Sasha were making a lot of noise last night.</u>

Eva: sorry. you/try/to sleep?

_____

Elena: no. I/not/sleep. I/read.

_____

Eva: well, first Sasha and I/watch/a great TV program.

_____

Elena: is that why/you/laugh/so hard?

_____

Eva: for part of the time. Later, we/laugh/because we/look at/some old pictures of you!

_____

MEANING AND USE

3 **Expressing Actions or States Completed in the Past**

A. Complete these questions with the most logical simple past ending from the choices in the *Time Clauses* box below.

> **TIME CLAUSES**
>
> before you had a car
>
> when you lived in the Caribbean
>
> when you were growing up
>
> while you were at college
>
> when you ate in that fancy restaurant
>
> after I gave you my number

1. How was the weather <u>when you lived in the Caribbean?</u>

2. What did you order _____

3. Why didn't you call me _____

4. What did you and your family do together at night _____

5. How did you get around _____

6. How did you pay your tuition _____

B. Look at the questions in part A. Match the questions with these responses.

_4_ **a.** We played games, talked, and watched TV.

_____ **b.** Sorry. I meant to, but I got busy.

_____ **c.** I had a seafood salad.

_____ **d.** I always borrowed money from my parents.

_____ **e.** It used to rain every afternoon.

_____ **f.** I usually took the bus.

C. Look again at the questions in part A. Which questions are asking about:

a. _1_____ actions or states that lasted a long period of time?

b. _____ actions that lasted a short period of time?

4 Contrasting the Simple Past and the Past Continuous

Complete this story with the simple past or past continuous forms of the verbs in parentheses. Use contractions when possible.

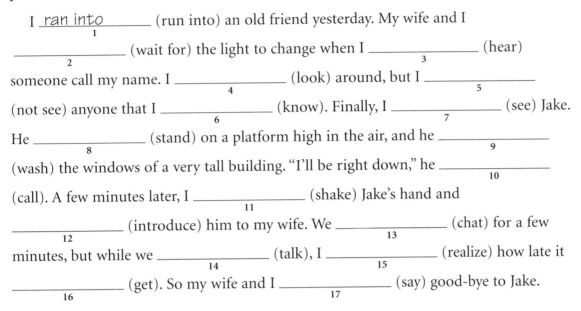

I _ran into_ (run into) an old friend yesterday. My wife and I
1

_____ (wait for) the light to change when I _____ (hear)
2   3

someone call my name. I _____ (look) around, but I _____
4   5

(not see) anyone that I _____ (know). Finally, I _____ (see) Jake.
6   7

He _____ (stand) on a platform high in the air, and he _____
8   9

(wash) the windows of a very tall building. "I'll be right down," he _____
10

(call). A few minutes later, I _____ (shake) Jake's hand and
11

_____ (introduce) him to my wife. We _____ (chat) for a few
12   13

minutes, but while we _____ (talk), I _____ (realize) how late it
14   15

_____ (get). So my wife and I _____ (say) good-bye to Jake.
16   17

5 Using the Simple Past and the Past Continuous in Time Clauses

A. Choose the correct clause to complete each sentence.

1. _____ , I always dreamt of working at the United Nations.

   a. When I grew up

   b. When I was growing up ⟵(circled)

2. When the fire alarm sounded, _____ .

   a. we were taking an important exam

   b. we took an important exam

3. The motorcycle came to a sudden stop _____ .

   a. after the driver saw a stop sign

   b. while the driver was seeing a stop sign

4. _____ , we all jumped.

   a. When the balloon was popping

   b. When the balloon popped

5. When the forest fire began near our town, _____ .

   a. almost everyone went to sleep

   b. most of the town was sleeping

6. _____ when I heard the noise.

   a. I was getting scared

   b. I got scared

B. Match each sentence in part A to its meaning below. Some of the sentences have more than one correct answer.

1. _d_   **a.** cause and effect

2. _____   **b.** sequential events

3. _____   **c.** an interrupted event

4. _____   **d.** action in progress over an extended period of time

5. _____   **e.** action in progress at an exact moment

6. _____

COMBINING FORM, MEANING, AND USE

Read each situation. Then choose the sentences that are true. Some of the situations have more than one correct answer.

1. He cut his foot before he mowed the lawn.

   (a.) After he cut his foot, he mowed the lawn.

   b. He cut his foot while he was mowing the lawn.

   (c.) First, he cut his foot. Then he moved the lawn.

2. I was shopping when I remembered my friend's birthday.

   a. I was shopping because it was my friend's birthday.

   b. I didn't remember my friend's birthday until I went shopping.

   c. While I was shopping, I realized it was my friend's birthday.

3. We were having a meeting when the boss arrived.

   a. First, the meeting started. Then the boss arrived.

   b. The meeting started before the boss arrived.

   c. The boss arrived. Then the meeting started.

4. Before she met Peter, she was dating a nice Spanish man.

   a. First, she went out with Peter. Then she met a Spanish man.

   b. She was seeing Peter when she met a Spanish man.

   c. She went out with a Spanish man before she met Peter.

5. The phone was ringing when I got to the door.

   a. I opened the door before the phone rang.

   b. The phone started ringing before I opened the door.

   c. After I opened the door, the phone started ringing.

6. When they built the new library, we didn't have to go downtown anymore.

   a. We went downtown before they built the new library.

   b. We didn't have to go downtown while they were building the new library.

   c. We didn't have to go downtown after they built the new library.

There are fourteen errors in this student's composition. The first one has been corrected. Find and correct thirteen more.

> I have
> ~~I'm having~~ so many wonderful memories of my childhood. While I was three years old, my family moved to Costa Rica. For the first few years, we lived in a small apartment. Then, when it's time for my brother and me to start school, my parents were buying our first house. For the first time, I had my own room and didn't had to share with my sister. I was loving that room! My mother was liking to sew, and she made a beautiful bedspread and matching curtains.
>
> We didn't have a lot of free time during the week, but weekends were always being a lot of fun. On Saturdays, we always play games together. Sunday was my favorite day because we almost always went to the beach. We were packing a big lunch, and Dad barbecue hamburgers or chicken. We kids were being sleepy after we were eating, so we spread blankets under a big tree and take naps.

On a separate sheet of paper, write a two-paragraph essay about a time when you first heard about an important event. Use the simple past and the past continuous when possible.

1. First, list some important world or family news to write about in your paragraphs.

   In the first paragraph, say what the event was and write about your situation when you heard the news. Where were you and what were you doing? Were you working, playing, studying? Were you alone or were you with other people?

2. In the second paragraph, write about your reactions to the news. What did you feel and think? Do you remember what you did later that day? How did the event affect your own life after that?

> I remember the night when the Anaheim Angels won the World Series. I was sitting in my room at my desk. I was studying for an important exam. My brother came in and told me . . . .

Future Forms

FORM

1 Examining Form

Read these interviews and complete the tasks below.

Lisa Rodriguez

Woman About Town

"The science magazines say
5 that there are going to be a lot
of medical breakthroughs.
For example, researchers will
be growing body parts, such
as hearts, livers, and hands in
10 labs and transplanting them
into people."—**Sam Leonard,
56, stockbroker**

"Because of global warming,
the climate will get a lot
15 warmer. People won't be
traveling to places like Hawaii
anymore to get away from the
cold." **–Marta Michaels, 37,
hairdresser**

Views of the Future

*Today our "Woman About Town" reporter, Lisa Rodriguez,
asked people on the street this question: What <u>will</u> things <u>be</u>
like thirty years from now?*

20 "The transportation system
will be really different. For
example, the taxis. Instead of
cars driving on the streets,
they'll be flying in the air. If
25 you want to go to the airport,
a flying taxi will come and
pick you up at your house."
**–Jorge Sanchez, 24,
postal worker**

30 "I think people and animals
will understand each other
better. Someone will invent a
new kind of language, and
people and animals will talk
35 with each other. That's
possible, don't you think?"
–Andrea Smith, 13, student

"Maybe I'm a pessimist, but
I think there's a fifty/fifty
40 chance that there will be a
big catastrophe. I think there
will be a big earthquake.
When that happens, a lot of
people will die." **–Robert
45 Grasso, 68, retired**

"What will things be like in
the future? I hope much
better, but how do I know?
My restaurant is going out of
50 business next week, and I
need to find another job. I
can't think about what I'll be
doing thirty years from now."
–Barbara Chu, 35, waitress

1. There are many examples of future forms in the interviews. The first one is underlined. Underline eight more.

2. Find a future time clause with *when* and circle it.

3. Check the correct statement about future time clauses.

_____ **a.** We use the simple present in the main clause and a different future form in the time clause.

_____ **b.** We use *will*, *be going to*, or a future continuous form in the main clause and the simple present in the time clause.

_____ **c.** A time clause always comes before the main clause.

Read the reasons Ben's friends can't come to his party on Saturday. Write sentences in the future continuous about what they will be doing instead.

1. **Ana and Miguel:** "We have tickets to a play downtown."

   Ana and Miguel will be watching a play downtown.
   _____

2. **Jane:** "I promised to teach my nieces how to bowl."

   _____

3. **David:** "I told my grandmother I'd go shopping with her."

   _____

4. **Takeshi:** "I have to help Jessica."

   _____

5. **Celia:** "I absolutely must catch up on my homework."

   _____

6. **Rachel:** "You won't believe it. I have to work!"

   _____

Look at the Independence Day Celebration poster. Then complete the conversation, using the simple present as future and the verbs *begin, cost, end, last,* and *start.*

Eric: When does the celebration begin?
      ₁
Bill: _____ on Friday at noon.
      ₂
Eric: _____
      ₃
Bill: _____ on Sunday night, after
      ₄
      the fireworks.

Eric: _____
      ₅
Bill: _____ on Saturday morning.
      ₆
      They're going to be exciting this year.

Eric: _____
      ₇
Bill: _____ all day Saturday and
      ₈
      half the day on Sunday.

Eric: _____
      ₉
Bill: _____ $5.00 a day for adults
      ₁₀
      and $2.50 for kids.

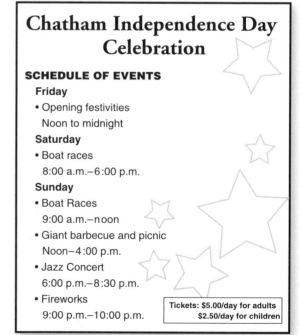

Chatham Independence Day Celebration

SCHEDULE OF EVENTS

Friday
- Opening festivities
  Noon to midnight

Saturday
- Boat races
  8:00 a.m.–6:00 p.m.

Sunday
- Boat Races
  9:00 a.m.–noon
- Giant barbecue and picnic
  Noon–4:00 p.m.
- Jazz Concert
  6:00 p.m.–8:30 p.m.
- Fireworks
  9:00 p.m.–10:00 p.m.

Tickets: $5.00/day for adults
$2.50/day for children

MEANING AND USE

4) **Contrasting Future Forms**

Choose one, two, or three correct phrases to complete each sentence.

1. It looks like _____ in a little while.
   a. it clears up
   b. it's going to clear up *(circled)*
   c. it's clearing up

2. _____ a party next Saturday?
   a. Do you have
   b. Are you going to have
   c. Are you having

3. I feel lucky. I think _____ the lottery this week.
   a. I'm winning
   b. I'm going to win
   c. I win

4. The meeting _____ at 2:30 on Friday.
   a. starts
   b. is starting
   c. is going to start

5. In the year 2025, our refrigerators _____ their own food.
   a. will order
   b. order
   c. are ordering

6. _____ into my new apartment on Saturday.
   a. I'm moving
   b. I move
   c. I'm going to move

5) **Ordering Events with Future Time Clauses**

Lisa has invited some friends over for dinner. Look at her TO DO list. Use the time word(s) in parentheses to write the order of things she's going to do before her guests arrive. Use *going to* in the main clause.

1. (when) <u>When she finishes work at the office,</u>
   <u>she's going to come home.</u>

2. (before) _____
   _____

3. (after) _____
   _____

4. (as soon as) _____
   _____

5. (until) _____
   _____

6. (after) _____
   _____

> **TO DO**
>
> 1. Come home. Finish work at the office.
>
> 2. Write down the grocery list. Go food shopping.
>
> 3. Take it out of the oven. Bake the turkey for 6 hours at 375°.
>
> 4. Polish the silver. Set the table.
>
> 5. Prepare all ingredients for the salad. Wait to add the dressing.
>
> 6. Wash the kitchen floor. Sweep the kitchen floor.

COMBINING FORM, MEANING, AND USE

Use each set of cues to write two conversations. Use the present continuous as future and the future with *going to* in each conversation.

1. **Hiro:** What/you/do/next Saturday?

    Koji: Yuko and I/spend/the day at the beach.

    a. **Hiro:** <u>What are you doing next Saturday?</u>

       Koji: <u>Yuko and I are going to spend the day at the beach.</u>

    b. **Hiro:** _____

       Koji: _____

2. **Ben:** When/you/finish/final exams?

    Kevin: I/finish/next week.

    a. **Ben:** _____

       Kevin: _____

    b. **Ben:** _____

       Kevin: _____

3. **David:** How/you/celebrate/your birthday this year?

    Kate: My parents/throw/me/a big party.

    a. **David:** _____

       Kate: _____

    b. **David:** _____

       Kate: _____

4. **Emily:** What/you/do/after graduation?

    Tony: I/leave/on a trip to Mexico.

    a. **Emily:** _____

       Tony: _____

    b. **Emily:** _____

       Tony: _____

There are nine errors in these paragraphs. The first one has been corrected. Find and correct eight more.

> *will have*
> People predict that genetic engineering ~~has~~ a major effect on our food supply in the future. Genetically engineered fruits, vegetables, and animals will help increase the food supply. For example, it is possible that people are growing tropical fruits such as bananas, coconuts, and pineapples in colder climates such as Canada or Russia. Foods on supermarket shelves are going taste better and last longer. Since these foods won't spoil as quickly, they are being abundant and cheap.
>
> These new foods also going to be better for you. Scientists manipulate the DNA of many foods to make them more nutritious and allergy-free. Potatoes will be having a special gene so that when people make French fries, they aren't soaking up as much oil. And there may even be special fruits and vegetables that act like vaccines. So instead of getting a shot to prevent disease, people are eating an apple or a carrot!

On a separate sheet of paper, write a paragraph about your vision of the future. Use the future with *will* and *going to*, the present continuous and the simple present as future, the future continuous, and future time clauses when possible.

Choose a time frame (such as 20 years from now) and answer these questions:

1. Will the world be a better place than it is now? Why or why not?

2. What kind of social changes will there be? What kind of work will people do? How will people spend their free time? How will they travel?

3. What will the environmental situation be like? Is there going to be more or less pollution? Will more animals be extinct?

> I think the world is probably going to be a better place in thirty years. There will be less poverty, and most people around the world will have enough to eat. At the same time, there will be more pollution . . . .

Chapters 1–3

A. Choose the correct clause to complete each sentence.

1. When I get home tonight, _____.
   a. I take a shower
   b. I took a shower
   c. I'm going to take a shower

2. Every day before she goes to work, _____.
   a. Barbara is feeding her cat
   b. Barbara feeds her cat
   c. Barbara was feeding her cat

3. I'm studying this semester, but _____.
   a. next year I look for a job
   b. next year I looked for a job
   c. next year I'll look for a job

4. Why didn't you take your umbrella _____?
   a. when it started to rain
   b. when it's starting to rain
   c. when it starts to rain

5. _____, my brother worked on his math assignment.
   a. While I was playing video games
   b. While I am playing video games
   c. While I play video games

6. As soon as I get my next paycheck, _____.
   a. I bought some new clothes
   b. I was buying some new clothes
   c. I'm going to buy some new clothes

7. Until _____, we can't take a trip.
   a. we save more money
   b. we'll save more money
   c. we saved more money

8. Today it's cloudy, and _____.
   a. the wind blows
   b. the wind is blowing
   c. the wind blew

9. I'll go home after _____.
   a. the game is going to be over
   b. the game is over
   c. the game will be over

10. _____ when I heard a loud noise.
    a. I will walk in the garden
    b. I walk in the garden
    c. I was walking in the garden

11. _____, please turn out the light.
    a. Before you are leaving the room
    b. Before you will leave the room
    c. Before you leave the room

12. _____ after you graduate from high school?
    a. What do you do
    b. What will you do
    c. What were you doing

13. _____ until you get back.
    a. I stay here
    b. I was staying here
    c. I'll stay here

14. Bill weighs too much, so _____.
    a. he decided to go on a diet
    b. he decides to go on a diet
    c. he decided to stop his diet

B. Find and correct the error in form, meaning, or use in each of these sentences.

15. How was the fire starting?

16. The children played in the yard when it started to rain.

17. The movie is about a group of teenagers who are getting lost in the forest.

18. I know these jeans are looking terrible, but all my other pants are in the laundry.

19. When Kedra was a child, she would have a lot of friends.

20. Marcus and I won't be getting marry next year because we just broke off our engagement.

21. The Chiefs will be the champions this year because they're definitely winning tomorrow night's game.

22. I promise that I will be finishing my homework.

23. If you have time, will you be stopping and pick up some bread on your way home?

24. Carlos is usually being very level-headed, but today he's overreacting to everything.

25. I was jogging in the park while I fell and hurt my left ankle.

C. Choose two **words or phrases** to complete each sentence.

26. Serena _____ a better player as she gets older.
    a. became   c. is becoming
    b. will become   d. becomes

27. When we were kids, we _____ understand the importance of getting enough sleep.
    a. don't   c. didn't
    b. couldn't   d. wouldn't

28. My tooth _____, so I think I will see a dentist.
    a. hurts   c. hurt
    b. is hurting   d. was hurting

29. What _____ when you saw the president?
    a. you did   c. did you
    b. were you doing d. did you do

30. We're happy they _____ a new supermarket on the corner.
    a. 're opening   c. open
    b. 'll open   d. opened

4 The Present Perfect

FORM

Read this article and complete the tasks below.

Finding a Way off the Streets

Alex Paga didn't plan to join the circus when he ran away from home at age eight. But he did—and it probably saved his life.

5 "If This Street Were Mine" is a program that uses circus arts to give the runaway and homeless children of Rio de Janeiro, Brazil, a second chance at life. Paga <u>has been</u> with the 10 program for over ten years, and he's now an acrobatics instructor.

Some 1,300 street children have gone through the program since it began in 1992, says its director, Cesar 15 Marques. Of the approximately 1,000 children the program has maintained contact with, only 200 have returned to the streets. Every year the program sends six children to the National 20 Circus School in Rio, and graduates have performed in countries from Argentina to Germany.

"If This Street Were Mine" performers

But Marques says the program isn't about turning children into clowns. It has succeeded at getting so many kids off the streets by building confidence and a 25 sense of responsibility. It seems that putting on shows teaches children to set goals and to accept tasks. In fact, some graduates of "If This Street Were Mine" who didn't make it as acrobats or clowns have found careers as mechanics or bricklayers. And that is something to smile about.

There are seven examples of verbs in the present perfect in the article. The first one is underlined. Underline six more.

Complete this conversation with the words in parentheses and the present perfect.
Use contractions when possible.

Kate: Where _have you been_ (you/be)?
1

Andre: Sorry we're late. We _____ (be) stuck in traffic for the past hour.
2

Kate: The traffic _____ (be) really awful lately, hasn't it?
3

Irina: You can say that again! So _____ (you/order) anything yet?
4

Kate: The waiter _____ (come) to the table several times since I got
5

here, but I _____ (not/order) anything because I wanted to wait
6

for you guys.

Irina: Well, I _____ (not/eat) all day, so I'm starving.
7

_____ (you/see) that waiter recently?
8

Kate: Yes. Here he comes now. Andre, you _____ (eat) here before.
9

What's good?

Andre: This is a great restaurant. I _____ (never/have) a bad meal here.
10

Everything's delicious.

Irina: It's a little expensive, though. We _____ (pay) at least fifteen
11

dollars for an entrée every time we _____ (have) dinner here.
12

Kate: Wow, you're right. Here's a pasta dish for eighteen dollars.

Irina: Hmm. They _____ (raise) the prices again. Look, Andre. That tuna
13

dish is twenty-five dollars now.

Waiter: Good evening. Well, I see you're all here now. _____ (you/decide)
14

what you'd like to order?

Andre: Uh . . . well, no, we haven't. I think we need a little more time.

Waiter: No problem. _____ (you/hear) about our specials tonight? They're
15

all very good! And we _____ (add) a new specialty to the menu—
16

chicken with a delicious mushroom sauce!

Irina: That sounds good. . . but how much does it cost?

MEANING AND USE

Read the information and complete the tasks below.

> ## Many Admit to Bending the Rules
>
> This poll shows the percentage of Americans who admit to doing the following at least once in their lives.
>
> - Driving faster than the speed limit 92%
> - Telling a white lie 89%
> - Calling in sick to work when they were healthy 67%
> - Parking illegally 60%
> - Cheating on an exam 57%
> - Writing a personal e-mail at work 43%
> - Making a long-distance phone call at work 38%
> - Cutting into a line 19%

A. Write eight statements about what Americans admit to doing at least once in their lives. Be sure to write out the percentages.

1. Ninety-two percent have driven faster than the speed limit.

2. _____

3. _____

4. _____

5. _____

6. _____

7. _____

8. _____

B. Look at the poll again. What questions were asked in the poll? Write the questions. Then write your own answers.

1. Q: Have you ever driven faster than the speed limit?

   A: Yes, I have. I've driven faster than the speed limit many times.

    OR   No, I haven't. I've never driven faster than the speed limit.

2. Q: _____

   A: _____

3. Q: _____

   A: _____

4. Q: _____

   A: _____

5. Q: _____

   A: _____

6. Q: _____

   A: _____

7. Q: _____

   A: _____

8. Q: _____

   A: _____

4 **Writing About Recent Past Time and Continuing Time up to Now**

Complete this story with *lately, recently, just, for,* and *since.* In some sentences, more than one answer is possible.

I've lived in the same house all my life. The Rosses have been our next-door

neighbors _for_____ almost ten years now. Amy Ross and I have been best
                1

friends _____ we were in junior high school. Amy and I used to be
              2

inseparable, but I haven't seen much of her _____ . Amy and her boyfriend,
                                                    3

Matt, have been very busy _____ . You see, Amy and Matt have
                                 4

_____ announced their engagement. They decided that they wanted to get
     5

married a few months ago, but they didn't tell anyone but me. I've kept their secret

_____ almost three months, and I'm very glad I don't have to keep the secret
     6

anymore. They've known each other _____ their first year in college, and
                                          7

they've been in love _____ five years. I miss my friend a lot these days, but
                            8

I'm really happy for her. I know that she and Matt will be very happy.

Gina and Steve are going to Argentina. They've made lists of things to do. Now they're asking each other about what they've done. Use the information in the lists and the cues in parentheses to write questions and responses.

Gina's "to do" list
✓ Renew passports
Pick up tickets at travel agency
Reserve a rental car
✓ Shop for summer clothes
Get film and toiletries
Type up itinerary

Steve's "to do" list
✓ Make plane reservations
✓ Choose a hotel in Buenos Aires
Pay the room deposit
✓ Buy travel insurance
✓ Shop for summer clothes

1. **Gina:** (make the plane reservations)

   Have you made the plane reservations yet?

   Steve: (yesterday)

   Yes, I have. I made them yesterday.

2. **Gina:** (choose a hotel in Buenos Aires)

   _____

   Steve: (the Olympic)

   _____

3. **Gina:** (pay the room deposit)

   _____

   Steve: (tomorrow)

   _____

4. **Steve:** (renew the passports)

   _____

   Gina: (on Wednesday)

   _____

5. **Steve:** (reserve a rental car)

   _____

   Gina: (too busy)

   _____

COMBINING FORM, MEANING, AND USE

Choose the correct ending for each sentence.

1. He does his job very well because
   a. he did it all his life.
   b. he's done it all his life.

2. We lived in Seattle for a few years,
   a. but we don't like it very much.
   b. but we didn't like it very much.

3. Hiro and Keiko were married for many years,
   a. and they had a very happy life together.
   b. and they've had a very happy life together.

4. I've washed these pants a million times,
   a. but they still look new.
   b. and they looked terrible.

5. I think the teacher is wrong. George Eliot, the nineteenth-century author,
   a. wrote more than three novels.
   b. has written more than three novels.

6. Some people think he was an excellent leader,
   a. but he's made a lot of mistakes during his presidency.
   b. but he made a lot of mistakes during his presidency.

7. The United States has never won the World Cup in soccer,
   a. but the team is improving in recent years.
   b. but the team has improved in recent years.

8. The headquarters of the United Nations has always been located in New York City,
   a. and most people think it's a good location for it.
   b. but most people thought it was a good location for it.

9. Last summer was the hottest one on record,
   a. but this summer has been even hotter.
   b. but we have had hotter summers.

10. Security in European airports has been strict for many years,
   a. and now it's become strict in the U.S.
   b. and now it became strict in the U.S.

On a separate sheet of paper, write two paragraphs about your travel experiences. Use present perfect and past forms when possible.

1. In the first paragraph, write about how much you have traveled in general. Answer these questions:

   • Have you traveled a lot?

   • What countries have you visited?

2. In the second paragraph, write about a place that you have visited more than once. Answer these questions:

   • How many times have you been there?

   • Have you always enjoyed going there?

   • What kinds of experiences have you had?

> I didn't travel much when I was a child, but since then I have traveled a lot. I have made several trips outside the country in the last five years . . . .

5 The Present Perfect Continuous

FORM

1 **Examining Form**

Read this magazine article and complete the tasks below.

What's Next for Steven Spielberg?

Moviegoers around the world $\boxed{\text{have been}}$ $\overset{\frown}{\text{looking}}$ forward to filmmaker Steven Spielberg's next film. What has he been working on these days? He hasn't discussed the details of his latest project, but judging
5 from the popularity and box-office success of his last several movies, he's been working with his usual creativity and passion.

Steven Spielberg

Steven Spielberg has been making films almost all his life. Born in 1947 in Cincinnati, Ohio, Spielberg
10 made his first film—thanks to his father's 8mm camera—when he was only 12. In 1970, he attracted attention with a short film that he made around the time he graduated from California State University, Long Beach. He became one of the youngest television directors at Universal Studios, and he was soon making
15 theatrically released motion pictures. His second film, *Jaws*, the thriller about a great white shark, has been frightening audiences since 1975. The string of hits that followed *Jaws*—including *E.T. the Extra-Terrestrial* (1982), the Academy Award-winning *Schindler's List* (1993), *Saving Private Ryan* (1998), and *Minority Report* (2002)—has made Steven Spielberg the most commercially successful director of
20 all time.

1. There are five examples of the present perfect continuous in the article. The first one is underlined. Underline four more.

2. Circle the main verb and draw a box around the two auxiliaries in the five examples. The first one is done for you.

Complete these conversations with the words in parentheses and the present perfect continuous. Use contractions when possible.

Conversation 1

Mother: Jenny, You've been on the phone all morning.

Who _have you been talking_ (you/talk) to?
₁

Daughter: I _____ (call) all my friends to tell them the good news about
₂

my scholarship.

Mother: Well, I hope no one _____ (try) to get through to me.
₃

I _____ (ask) you to get off the phone since 10:00. I'm
₄

expecting an important call.

Conversation 2

Ben: We haven't seen much of Kate lately. _____ (she/avoid) us?
₁

Teresa: Of course not. It's just that she _____ (work) overtime a lot.
₂

She _____ (get) home really late, so she _____
₃ ₄

(not/do) much besides work and sleep.

Ben: I hope she _____ (take care) of herself so she doesn't ruin
₅

her health.

Conversation 3

Interviewer: So the Olympics start tomorrow. How long _____
₁

(you/plan) for this event?

Sarah: I _____ (prepare) for the Olympics my entire life, and my
₂

parents _____ (make) sacrifices for years to help give me this
₃

opportunity.

Interviewer: And we _____ (watch) you for years. You _____
₄ ₅

(improve) your form and speed over the years, and you

_____ (skate) beautifully lately. The gold medal has your
₆

name on it!

Sarah: I hope you're right.

MEANING AND USE

Write sentences in the present perfect continuous about the situations below. Use *just, recently,* and *lately* when possible and join sentences with *and* or *because.* Use the phrases in the box.

> go to parties/study enough
>
> sleep well/have nightmares
>
> eat too much/exercise enough
>
> go straight home after work/go to the hospital to visit her uncle
>
> not spend time with friends/paint their house
>
> talk to his grandmother/not feel well

1. Julie used to be very fit, but she's gained a lot of weight.

   She's been eating too much lately, and she hasn't been

   exercising enough.

2. Paulo has always been a good student, but suddenly he isn't doing well in school.

   _____

   _____

3. Rick looks worried.

   _____

   _____

4. Kim has trouble staying awake at work.

   _____

   _____

5. The Normans usually have guests during the weekend, but they haven't had company for over a month.

   _____

   _____

6. Rita has been getting home from work later than usual.

   _____

   _____

Choose the correct sentence to complete the conversations.

1. **Nancy:** That's a new skirt you're wearing, isn't it?

   Emily: _____
   a. This? I wore it for years.
   b. This? I've been wearing it for years.

2. **Paulo:** _____

   Pedro: I finished it last night.
   a. Have you finished the book yet?
   b. Have you returned the book?

3. **Alex:** _____

   Luisa: Yes, I have.
   a. Have you ever traveled to Italy?
   b. Did you go to Italy?

4. **Lee:** Do you see Chris a lot?

   Matt: _____
   a. Yes, I've seen him twice this week.
   b. Yes, I've met him.

5. **Carlos:** _____

   Hector: About twenty minutes.
   a. How long have you waited for me?
   b. How long have you been waiting for me?

6. **Irina:** At last! Some sunshine!

   Andre: I know. _____
   a. It's been raining all day.
   b. It just started to rain.

7. **Mrs. Ruiz:** _____

   Mr. Ruiz: Aren't they finished yet?
   a. The Carters have redecorated their apartment.
   b. The Carters have been redecorating their apartment.

8. **Satomi:** So what are we going to do?

   Tomiko: I'm not sure. _____
   a. I haven't decided.
   b. I haven't been deciding.

5 **Contrasting the Present Perfect Continuous with Other Verb Forms**

Complete these conversations with the words in parentheses and the present perfect continuous, the present perfect, or the simple past. In some sentences, more than one form is acceptable. Use contractions when possible.

Conversation 1

Celia: _Have you heard_ (you/hear) from Kevin lately? I _____ (think) about
          ¹   ²
   him a lot recently.

Luisa: I _____ (not/speak) to him for ages, but he _____ (call)
              ³   ⁴
   Diane last week. Apparently, he _____ (travel) in Asia for business,
                                        ⁵
   but he'll be back on Saturday. Diane _____ (promise) to pick him up
                                            ⁶
   at the airport.

Conversation 2

Keiko: _____ (you/read) this article?

               1

Yuko: No, I _____ (not/see) that magazine yet.

               2

Keiko: Well, it says here that Winona Ryder _____ (make) films since she was

                                           3

        12 years old.

Yuko: Yes, I _____ (know) that. She _____ (work) in films for

                 4   5

        over half her life. But you know, I _____ (not/see) her in a movie in

                                         6

        ages. _____ (she/work) much lately?

               7

Keiko: It says here that she _____ (take) some time off, but she's starting a new

                                  8

        film next year.

Yuko: That's good news. I _____ (love) her last film.

                       9

COMBINING FORM, MEANING, AND USE

6 Thinking About Meaning and Use

Choose two possible responses to complete each conversation.

1. **Gary:** Hanna just called. She's been sitting in traffic for over an hour.

   Peter: _____
   - **a.** I guess she's going to be late.
   - **b.** So that's why she was so late!
   - **c.** That's why she's been getting here late.
   - **d.** That's so frustrating!

2. **Lisa:** Oh, look. It's been raining.

   Sarah: _____
   - **a.** Don't forget your umbrella.
   - **b.** Try not to step in the puddles.
   - **c.** I'm glad it stopped.
   - **d.** You're right. It is.

3. **Yuji:** I've just been reading an interesting article about whales.

   Satomi: _____
   - **a.** Can I read it when you're done?
   - **b.** What does it say?
   - **c.** When did you write it?
   - **d.** Who's been writing it?

4. **Man:** How long have you been selling used cars?

   Car Dealer: _____
   - **a.** Six years ago.
   - **b.** Six so far.
   - **c.** For about a year.
   - **d.** Since 1998.

5. **Hector:** What's Carlos been doing lately?

   Silvio: _____
   - **a.** Taking lots of courses.
   - **b.** He's just studied really hard.
   - **c.** He's a full-time student these days.
   - **d.** He's fine.

6. **Father:** Has Sarah been having problems at school?

   Mother: _____
   - **a.** Yes, she has. She's very upset.
   - **b.** No, she isn't. Everything's fine.
   - **c.** No, but she's been working really hard.
   - **d.** Yes, she has been there.

There are nine errors in this text. The first one has been corrected. Find and correct eight more.

The History of Soccer

Soccer is the most popular international team sport. Historians believe that people ~~has~~ *have* been playing soccer since the year 217 A.D., when the first game has been part of a victory celebration in England. Soccer became popular in Europe over the centuries, and eventually it spread throughout most of the world. In the United States, soccer has always been being secondary to American football. Recently, however, soccer has growing in popularity.

In 1904, several nations have formed the International Federation of Football (FIFA), which has been regulating international competition since over a century. Since 1930, the World Cup have been bringing countries together. And although women weren't playing soccer for as long as men have, an important international event, the Women's World Cup, has been taken place every four years since 1991.

On a separate sheet of paper, write two paragraphs about an activity that you have been involved in for several years. It could be learning English or an academic subject, or a sport or favorite pastime, such as playing soccer or playing a musical instrument. Use the present perfect continuous, the present perfect, and the simple past when possible.

1. In the first paragraph, write about how long you have been doing this activity and describe your feelings about it in general.

2. In the second paragraph, write about your experience in more detail. Answer questions such as these:

- Have you been doing this activity continuously over the years, or have you done it for a short time, then stopped, then started again, etc.?

- Have you improved or learned quickly enough?

- Have you ever felt frustrated with your progress?

- What "lessons" have you learned that might be interesting to another person interested in that subject or activity?

> Playing soccer is one of my favorite activities. I have been playing soccer ever since I was five years old. I like it because . . . .

The Past Perfect and the Past Perfect Continuous

FORM

1 Examining Form

Read this excerpt from a romance novel and complete the tasks below.

Julie <u>had been walking</u> for hours when she suddenly noticed that the sun was sinking low in the sky. She (had lost track) of time because she had been thinking about the most important decision she'd ever had to make in her life.

Things hadn't been the same between Julie and her fiance, David, since he accepted
5 a job in Paris. They had known each other for almost five years, and in that time, they had never argued much. Lately, though, their relationship had become stormy. They seemed to be finding fault with each other and disagreeing about everything. For the first time, she was starting to wonder if she was ready for marriage. And with the wedding only twenty days away, she needed to make up her mind soon.

10 Everything in Julie's life had been going well until her world fell apart just a month before. A large company had offered David an important position that would require him to move to France. As his wife, Julie would have to go, too. Why hadn't he discussed his decision with her?

Although Julie had always wanted to live abroad, she felt very confused. Was she
15 ready to move halfway across the world, leaving behind her friends and family and the only home she had ever known? If the answer was no, was she ready to say goodbye to the only man she had ever loved?

1. There are three examples of the past perfect continuous in the story. The first one is underlined. Underline two more.

2. There are many examples of the past perfect. The first one is circled. Circle six more.

3. How are the past perfect and the past perfect continuous different in form? Check all the correct statements below. Correct the incorrect statements.

_____ a. The past perfect uses two auxiliaries.

_____ b. The past perfect continuous uses two auxiliaries.

_____ c. Both the past perfect and the past perfect continuous use *have* or *has* to form contractions, negative statements, and short answers.

2 Working on the Past Perfect

Before Stefan went away to college, he had never done these things. Write sentences about Stefan, using the words in parentheses and the past perfect.

Before this year,

1. (cook his own meals) _he had never cooked his own meals._

2. (wash his own dishes) _____

3. (make his own bed) _____

4. (do his own laundry) _____

3 Practicing the Past Perfect Continuous

A community group organized a project to clean up a park. How long had the group been working when the people below came to help? Look at the list and write sentences in the past perfect continuous.

```
RIVERSIDE PARK CLEANUP SCHEDULE

 9:00-10:00   pick up the trash
10:00-10:30   pull weeds
10:30-11:00   wash the benches
11:00-12:00   paint the benches
12:00-12:30   clean the playground
12:30- 1:00   rake leaves
```

1. Ana got there at 9:15. _When Ana got there, the group had been_
   picking up the trash for fifteen minutes.

2. Chris and Emily arrived at 10:25. _____
   _____

3. Sasha came at 10:35. _____
   _____

4. Jane got there at 11:30. _____
   _____

5. Mr. and Mrs. Rivera came at 12:20. _____
   _____

6. Rick arrived at 12:45. _____
   _____

The Past Perfect and the Past Perfect Continuous   37

MEANING AND USE

Look at the timeline of Pablo Picasso's life. Then read each pair of sentences about Picasso and combine them, using the adverb in parentheses and the past perfect.

```
                         PABLO PICASSO

  ┌ 1881   was born in Málaga, Spain
  ├ 1882   drew his first picture
  ├ 1883   spoke his first word
  ├ 1897   entered the Royal Academy in Madrid
  ├ 1904   had created over 1,000 paintings and drawings
  ├ 1904   moved to Paris
  ├ 1907   painted Les Demoiselles d'Avignon
  ├ 1914   became well known
  ├ 1937   Guernica, Spain bombed by the Nazis
  ├ 1937   painted anti-war painting Guernica
  ├ 1947   moved to southern France
  ├ 1954   met Jacqueline Roque
  ├ 1961   married Jacqueline Roque
  └ 1973   died in Mougins, France
```

1. Picasso drew his first picture.

   Picasso turned two. (by the time)

   Picasso had drawn his first picture by the time he turned two. OR

   By the time he turned two, Picasso had drawn his first picture.

2. Picasso spoke his first word.

   Picasso drew his first picture. (before)

   _____

   _____

3. Picasso lived in Málaga.

   Picasso entered the Royal Academy in Madrid. (until)

   _____

   _____

4. Picasso was 23 years old.

   Picasso produced more than 1,000 works of art. (by the time)

   _____

   _____

5. Picasso became well known.

   Picasso moved to Paris. (after)

   _____

   _____

6. Picasso painted *Les Demoiselles d'Avignon*.

   The history of art changed forever. (after)

   _____

   _____

7. The Nazis bombed Guernica, Spain.

   Picasso painted his anti-war painting, *Guernica*. (after)

   _____

   _____

8. Picasso moved to southern France.

   Picasso lived in Paris for many years. (when)

   _____

   _____

9. Picasso and Jacqueline Roque got married.

   Jacqueline Roque was Picasso's companion for seven years. (before)

   _____

   _____

10. Picasso lived in Mougins for almost 20 years.

    Picasso died. (when)

    _____

    _____

A. The community group from Exercise 3 continued working after lunch. Look at their plans for the afternoon.

```
FINAL RIVERSIDE PARK CLEANUP SCHEDULE

 9:00-10:00   pick up the trash      2:00-2:30   cut the grass
10:00-10:30   pull weeds             2:30-3:30   trim the trees
10:30-11:00   wash the benches       3:30-4:30   plant flowers
11:00-12:00   paint the benches      4:30-5:00   empty the trash
12:00-12:30   clean the playground               cans
12:30-1:00    rake leaves
 1:00-2:00    LUNCH
```

B. Write sentences describing what the group had already done and what they hadn't done yet when the following people got to the park. Use the past perfect with *already* and *not . . . yet* and the words in parentheses.

1. Nancy arrived at 10:30. (pick up the trash/wash the benches)

   The group had already picked up the trash, but they hadn't washed

   the benches yet.

2. Susan and Jeff got there at 11:00. (cut the grass/pull weeds)

   _____

   _____

3. The Castro family arrived at 12:00. (rake leaves/pick up the trash)

   _____

   _____

4. Diane and Eric arrived at 3:30. (plant flowers/trim the trees)

   _____

   _____

5. The Hassan family arrived at 4:30. (empty the trash cans/plant flowers)

   _____

   _____

Expressing Reasons and Contrasts

Match the different words or phrases from each column to write twelve logical
sentences with the past perfect and the past perfect continuous.

		I'd been working at the computer for hours.
		I'd left my glasses at home.
		my old one had been running fine.
I bought a new car		I hadn't worked very hard on it.
My eyes were aching		I'd been studying very hard.
My teacher loved my report	although	I'd taken a nap after lunch.
My grades were terrible	because	I hadn't been taking good class notes lately.
I'd never bought a new car		I'd never had enough money.
I got a low grade on my report		my parents had always promised to help with the payments.
		my old one had been acting up.

1. I bought a new car although my old one had been running fine.

2. _____

3. _____

4. _____

5. _____

6. _____

7. _____

8. _____

9. _____

10. _____

11. _____

12. _____

COMBINING FORM, MEANING, AND USE

7 Thinking About Meaning and Use

Choose two possible endings to each sentence.

1. We didn't see Bill at the party because
   a. he'd left before we arrived.
   b. he left after we got there.
   c. he got there after we'd left.
   d. we arrived before he went home.

2. Maria got a terrible sunburn
   a. because she had used plenty of sunscreen.
   b. even though she had stayed in the shade.
   c. although she hadn't used sunscreen.
   d. because she'd spent the day at the beach.

3. I'd been driving for hours,
   a. but I'm not ready to stop.
   b. and I'd never felt so tired.
   c. and I was starting to feel sleepy.
   d. so the car has run out of gas.

4. By the time the police came,
   a. an ambulance took the man to the hospital.
   b. a large crowd of people had gathered.
   c. the firefighters have put out the fire.
   d. we'd all managed to get out of the car.

5. Eric had been sleeping late
   a. before he got this job.
   b. after he got this job.
   c. because he was tired from work.
   d. although he was tired from work.

6. Rachel had never seen a live tiger
   a. after she went to the zoo.
   b. before she went to India.
   c. until she traveled to Africa.
   d. when she'd gone on safari.

8 Writing

On a separate sheet of paper, write a three-paragraph story about a recent event in the lives of two people (husband and wife, boyfriend and girlfriend, people in a family). Follow the format of the story in Exercise 1. Use the past perfect, the past perfect continuous, the simple past, and time clauses to describe the setting and to explain the story.

1. In paragraph 1, introduce one of the people. Where is that person, and what is he or she thinking about?
2. In paragraph 2, introduce the second person and talk about the event. How has that event affected the relationship?
3. In paragraph 3, talk about the person's feelings and how the person plans to deal with the event.

> Jake had been driving in the rain for over an hour when suddenly he realized what he had to do. Over the past two weeks, he had tried too hard to control the situation. Now . . . .

Chapters 4–6

A. Use the cues to write sentences with the verb form in parentheses. If you can't write a correct sentence with that verb form, write (✕). Use contractions when possible. Then answer the question about each group of sentences.

> How long / the police / try / to solve that crime ?

1. _____

   (present perfect continuous)

2. _____

   (past perfect continuous)

3. _____

   (present perfect)

4. _____

   (simple past)

5. *In which sentence(s) are the police no longer trying to solve the crime?* _____

> We / shop / at that store for years .

6. _____

   (past perfect)

7. _____

   (simple past)

8. _____

   (present perfect continuous)

9. *In which sentence(s) is the store probably out of business?* _____

They / have / that car since 1998 .

10. _____

(present perfect)

11. _____

(past perfect)

12. _____

(present perfect continuous)

13. _____

(past perfect continuous)

14. _____

(simple past)

15. *In which sentence(s) do they still have the car?* _____

B. Match each sentence with the response below.

_____ **16.** I've been working out for over an hour.

_____ **17.** My parents had been living in the same house since 1980.

_____ **18.** We hadn't been waiting long for Lee and Kalysa when they came.

_____ **19.** I'd been exercising for almost two hours.

_____ **20.** Have you always wanted to be a doctor?

_____ **21.** My family has lived in the same house since I was born.

_____ **22.** When I looked out the window, I saw that it had rained.

---

a. I'm surprised you didn't hear the rain. It didn't rain for long, but it was loud.

b. No, I wanted to be a lawyer.

c. Why did they move?

d. You were lucky, because they're usually late.

e. Aren't you exhausted?

f. They'll probably live there forever.

g. I'm sure you were exhausted.

C. Check (✓) the sentences that are correct. Write (x) next to the sentences that have errors in form or meaning and use and rewrite them.

23. _____ Jenny has been walking for hours when she noticed it was late.

_____

_____

24. _____ I didn't see Rosa because she'd left before I arrived.

_____

_____

25. _____ Yuji is been cooking all day for the party.

_____

_____

26. _____ Until we went to France last summer, we've never eaten snails. They're delicious!

_____

_____

27. _____ Gary has been in love with Kate since he first saw her.

_____

_____

28. _____ Alex won the perfect-attendance award because he hadn't been missing a day since school started.

_____

_____

29. _____ The American Revolutionary War had lasted from 1775 to 1783.

_____

_____

30. _____ By the time we got to the Grand Canyon, we'd been driving for ten hours.

_____

_____

7 Modals of Possibility

FORM

Read this magazine article and complete the tasks below.

Computer Viruses Can Strike at Any Time

Victor decided to check his e-mail once more before he left the office for the day. He <u>might</u> have a reply from his supervisor about the two personal days that he wanted to take the following week. When he looked, there was only one message in his mailbox. The subject line read ILOVEYOU. "Who could that be from?" thought Victor, who rarely
5 received personal e-mail at work. "Someone's got to be playing a joke," he decided as he double-clicked on the attached document. Too late! Victor had just opened a file containing a dangerous computer virus that was later referred to as the Love Bug. Less than a second later, everything on Victor's hard drive had disappeared.

A deadly virus like the Love Bug could strike at any time. So how do we protect
10 ourselves? Here is some advice from the experts:
 • Don't open e-mail from strangers. That message from "A FRIEND" might contain a virus that could cause you major headaches.
 • Back up important files on a regular basis. That way, it should be easy to replace them if a virus wipes out your hard drive.
15 • Install the latest anti-virus software. It may not be possible to protect your computer against every brand-new virus, but keeping your software up to date ought to give you some peace of mind.

---

back up: make a copy of
double-clicked: clicked twice with a mouse
hard drive: the part of a computer that stores information

install: make ready for use
subject line: topic of message
wipes out: destroys

---

1. There are many examples of modals and phrasal modals in the article. The first one is underlined. Underline six more. Some will be used more than once.

2. What follows the modals? Check all the correct answers below.

   _____ **a.** base form of the main verb

   _____ **b.** infinitive of the main verb

   _____ **c.** *be* + verb + *ing*

Working on Modals of Possibility

Check each sentence for the correct form of the modals and phrasal modals of possibility and probability. If the sentence is incorrect, correct it.

	CORRECT	INCORRECT
1. Blind dates must ~~not~~ be very nerve-wracking.		✓
2. This article has to be correct.		
3. I mayn't be in class tomorrow.		
4. They should be here by now.		
5. Should the accused man be innocent?		
6. This hasn't got to be right. It makes no sense.		
7. Could these keys be Amy's? Yes, they could be.		
8. Steve must feels terrible about this.		

3 **Completing a Dialogue with Modals of Possibility**

Complete these conversations using the words in parentheses. Use contractions when possible.

Conversation 1

   Koji: It's almost 8:00. Where _could Alex be_ (Alex/be/could)?
   ⎯⎯⎯⎯⎯⎯⎯⎯1⎯⎯⎯⎯⎯⎯⎯⎯

Tomiko: He really ⎯⎯⎯⎯⎯⎯⎯2⎯⎯⎯⎯⎯⎯⎯ (be/ought to) here by now.

   Koji: Well, ⎯⎯⎯⎯⎯⎯⎯3⎯⎯⎯⎯⎯⎯⎯ (he/be/can/not) sick. I spoke to him a little while
   ago, and he was fine.

Tomiko: He ⎯⎯⎯⎯⎯⎯⎯4⎯⎯⎯⎯⎯⎯⎯ (be/may) stuck in traffic. Let's wait a few more
   minutes.

   Koji: If we wait much longer, ⎯⎯⎯⎯⎯⎯⎯5⎯⎯⎯⎯⎯⎯⎯ (we/miss/might) the beginning
   of the movie. Oh, there's the phone. ⎯⎯⎯⎯⎯⎯⎯6⎯⎯⎯⎯⎯⎯⎯ (that/be/have to) Alex.

Tomiko: I hope so, but where ⎯⎯⎯⎯⎯⎯⎯7⎯⎯⎯⎯⎯⎯⎯ (he/be/call/could) from?

   Koji: He just got a cell phone. ⎯⎯⎯⎯⎯⎯⎯8⎯⎯⎯⎯⎯⎯⎯ (he/be/call/must) from his car.

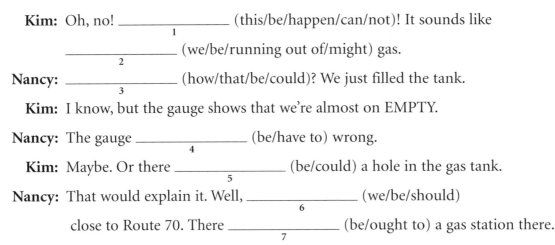

Conversation 2

Kim: Oh, no! _____ (this/be/happen/can/not)! It sounds like
1

_____ (we/be/running out of/might) gas.
2

Nancy: _____ (how/that/be/could)? We just filled the tank.
3

Kim: I know, but the gauge shows that we're almost on EMPTY.

Nancy: The gauge _____ (be/have to) wrong.
4

Kim: Maybe. Or there _____ (be/could) a hole in the gas tank.
5

Nancy: That would explain it. Well, _____ (we/be/should)
6

close to Route 70. There _____ (be/ought to) a gas station there.
7

MEANING AND USE

4 **Expressing Degrees of Certainty**

Read these sentences and complete the task below.

1. The cake ought to be ready. It's been in the oven for an hour.

2. There may be life on Mars, but most scientists doubt it.

3. She could have the flu, or she could just be tired.

4. There must be an easier way to clean this floor. Let's try using a brush.

5. Tony might be right about the court date.

6. This number can't be right. There's no such area code as 123.

7. David couldn't be guilty of such a terrible crime. I've known him all his life, and he wouldn't hurt a fly.

8. That's got to be Diane Waters's laptop. The screen says "Welcome, Diane."

9. This must be the house. I'm pretty sure that's Gary's car parked in front.

10. It's really sunny out this morning. It should be a beautiful day.

In the sentences above, find the following:

a. three examples that express a guess about a present situation (little certainty):
   2, _____

b. two examples that express an expectation about the present (some certainty):

   _____

c. three examples that draw a conclusion (strong certainty): _____

d. two examples that express the belief that something is impossible (strong

   certainty): _____

Complete the conversations with appropriate modals. Use *could, might* or *may* (little certainty); *should* and *ought to* (some certainty); or *must, have to,* or *have got to* (strong certainty). In some of the sentences, more than one answer is possible.

1. **Elena:** Are the cookies done yet?

   Teresa: They _might_ be. The recipe says to bake them for twelve to fifteen minutes, and they've been in the oven for almost fourteen.

2. **Amy:** Aren't you worried about the traffic?

   Susan: Not really. It's only 3:00, so the traffic _____ be pretty good.

3. **Satomi:** I found these keys on the sofa. Are they yours?

   Keiko: No, but they _____ be Yuko's. I've found her keys there before.

4. **Chris:** Whose comic books are these?

   Matt: They _____ belong to Jeff. He's the only one we know who still buys comics.

5. **Ana:** We saw Rosa and Paulo at the movies last night. They were holding hands. Are they dating?

   Jane: They _____ be. Rosa told me she had a new boyfriend, but I didn't know it was Paulo!

6. **Kate:** There's someone at the door.

   Ben: That _____ be Tony. He was going to try to stop by on his way home.

7. **Silvio:** Do you think they've developed our film yet?

   Luisa: The pictures _____ be ready by now. They promised to have them for us yesterday.

8. **Rick:** Is this Gary's house?

   Steve: It _____ be. That's Gary's car parked in the driveway.

9. **Chen:** I don't have a watch. What time is it?

   Lee: It _____ be just after 8 P.M. because the sun is setting now.

10. **Keon:** Do you know the name of that beautiful girl in the red dress?

    Marcus: It _____ be Jada. I think I met her once.

Rewrite the sentences. Use *could*, *might*, or *may* (little certainty); *should(n't)* and *ought to* (some certainty); or *will* or *won't* (strong certainty). There may be more than one correct answer.

1. It's very likely that it will be clear today.

   It should be clear today. OR It ought to be clear today.

2. There's a good chance that it will be cooler tonight.

   _____

3. It's possible that it will rain tomorrow.

   _____

4. There's a small chance that it will be warmer on Thursday.

   _____

5. There isn't any chance that it will snow on Saturday.

   _____

6. It's definite that the temperature will drop tomorrow.

   _____

COMBINING FORM, MEANING, AND USE

Read each situation and look at the pair of sentences that follow. Write *S* if the two sentences have the same meaning. Write *D* if their meanings are different. For the sentences that are different, change the *b* sentence so that it means the same as *a*.

_D_ 1. Tony almost never takes medicine, but he just took two aspirin.

   a. He must have a really bad headache.

   b. He might have a really bad headache.

   He's got to OR _He has to have a really bad headache._

____ 2. Mary lost her job today.

   a. She must be upset.

   b. She might be upset.

   _____

_____ 3. You should probably start dinner without me.

    a. I may be late tonight.

    b. I will be late tonight.

_____ 4. I haven't heard from Sarah in over a week.

    a. She's got to be really busy.

    b. She must be really busy.

_____ 5. The sky is getting very dark.

    a. It could rain any minute.

    b. It should rain any minute.

_____ 6. We're still making our vacation plans.

    a. We may go to Hawaii.

    b. We might go to Hawaii.

_____ 7. I heard a strange rumor about Koji today.

    a. It couldn't be true.

    b. It can't be true.

_____ 8. We're going to the Santana concert tonight.

    a. It should be great.

    b. It may be great.

_____ 9. There's the sign: "Bill's Diner."

    a. This has to be the place.

    b. This ought to be the place.

_____ 10. I'm not exactly sure where Kevin is, but

    a. he might be in his room.

    b. he could be in his room.

There are nine errors in this student's e-mail. The first one has been corrected. Find and correct eight more.

To: Lanita Carter
From: Matt Kennedy
Cc:
Subject: next week

Hi, Dr. Carter. I'm writing to tell you that I probably ~~mightn't~~ *won't* be in class next week. My

grandfather may needs an operation, and my parents want me to come home to be with the

family. No one has told me yet what kind of surgery Grandpa needs, but it should be serious.

Otherwise, my family wouldn't be suggesting that I make the long trip home. You'll may find this

a bit unusual, but I'm very close to my grandfather. I know this absence could to put my grade in

danger, but I'll work very hard so that I don't fall behind.

You mayn't be very happy about this, but I need to ask a special favor. Do you think you might

being able to e-mail me next week's assignments? That way, I maybe able to do some of them

while I'm away. I'm not sure, but I should am getting back to Los Angeles by April 1.

Thank you very much.

Matt Kennedy

---

9 **Writing**

On a separate sheet of paper, write a two- or three-paragraph letter to someone — a teacher, a friend, a relative, or your boss. Follow these steps:

1. Think of a situation where you are supposed to do something in the future but can't. Make notes for a letter in which you explain why.

2. Use your notes to write your letter. Remember to express your ideas with the correct verb tenses and present and future modals of possibility.

> I wanted to tell you why I won't be able to lend you my
>
> car next week. I have to make a short business trip . . . .

8 Past Modals

FORM

1 Examining Form

Read this excerpt from a history book and complete the tasks below.

Mystery in Malta

The small Mediterranean island of Malta is covered with grooves–thick lines that cut into the bare rocks, some as deep as 24 inches (600 mm). They run in pairs across the landscape and disappear into fields, roads, or houses, over cliffs and even into the sea.

5   Where <u>could</u> these grooves <u>have come</u> from? One theory was that the grooves were used to drain water. Experts decided to rule this out, however. The grooves <u>couldn't have been</u> part of a drainage system because they show no sign of water erosion.

Another possibility is that the grooves <u>may have been</u> an ancient civilization's 10   transportation system. Although wheeled vehicles <u>couldn't have used</u> them because the pairs of grooves are not exactly parallel, some archaeologists think that a type of primitive sled <u>must have provided</u> transportation for the inhabitants of Malta in about 2000 B.C. The problem with this theory: Who or what <u>could have pulled</u> the sleds? Animal hooves <u>would have worn</u> down the 15   rock, and even bare feet <u>would</u> probably <u>have polished</u> the surface. But apart from the grooves themselves, there aren't any other marks. The "Maltese Mystery" continues to fascinate both archaeologists and tourists.

1. There are eight examples of past modals in the excerpt. The first one is underlined. Underline seven more.

2. Check the correct statements about past modals.

　　✗ **a.** Past modals have only one form with all subjects.

　　_____ **b.** Past modals have this form:

　　　modal + *have* + past participle of main verb.

2 Working on Past Modals

Rewrite these sentences, using the past modal form. Use the time expressions in parentheses. Make all necessary changes.

1. I should take a coat to the game tonight. (last night)

   I should have taken a coat to the game last night.

2. I could pick you up at the airport tomorrow. (last weekend)

   I could

3. The students might not understand everything on today's test. (yesterday's)

   _____

4. David must be at the office right now. (yesterday afternoon)

   _____

5. We could go to the mountains this summer. (last summer)

   _____

6. There may be a lot of traffic this afternoon. (this morning)

   _____

7. The company might solve its financial problems this year. (last year)

   _____

8. You shouldn't stay up late tonight. (last night)

   _____

3 Completing Conversations with Past Modals

Complete these conversations using the words in parentheses. Use contractions when possible.

Conversation 1

Kedra: Eva _should have been_ (be/should) here an hour ago. She's never late.

   What _____ (happen/could) to her?

Jane: She _____ (might/not/receive) my message. I called to tell

   her we were coming here instead of going to Sugar and Spice. She

   _____ (must/go) to Sugar and Spice.

54   Chapter 8

Conversation 2

Derek: The police think they _____ (might/catch) the
1
Boonton Burglar.

Keon: It's about time! They _____ (should/got) him months ago.
2
It _____ (should/not/take) this long. That guy
3
_____ (had to/be/laughing) at the police since he started
4
robbing houses.

MEANING AND USE

4 **Using Modals of Past Possibility**

Read these sentences about "unexplained mysteries." Then rewrite the ideas, using
modals of past possibility and the cues in parentheses. In each sentence more than
one modal is possible.

1. Amelia Earhart was the first woman to fly across the Atlantic. She tried to fly around the world
   but disappeared. Did she have an accident, or is that just what she wanted people to think?

   a. She landed safely on an island and lived there. (guess)

   She might have/could have/may have landed safely on an island and

   lived there.

   b. She secretly returned to the United States. (guess)

   _____

   c. She ran out of fuel and crashed. (logical conclusion)

   _____

2. Stonehenge is a group of prehistoric stones in England. No one is sure what it is or
   why it was built.

   a. The builders traveled over land and sea to bring the stones for the monument.
   (logical conclusion)

   _____

   b. The building of the monument didn't start before 3000 B.C. (unlikely or
   impossible)

   _____

   c. The structure was a temple. (guess)

   _____

Imagine that some students told the class they had these experiences. Write two sentences giving your response, the first one expressing disbelief. Use the modals in parentheses.

1. "We saw Elvis Presley last night." (could, must)

   a. _They couldn't have seen Elvis because he's been dead for many years._

   b. _They must have seen someone who looked like Elvis._

2. "We've finished the homework." (could, may/start)

   a. _____

   b. _____

3. "The trip from New York to Washington, D.C., takes about three hours by train. We got there in less than an hour." (can, might/less than three hours)

   a. _____

   b. _____

4. "Rick robbed the bank."
   (could, someone else/must)

   a. _____

   b. _____

5. "We won a million dollars in the Publisher's Contest. We didn't receive an advertisement." (can, must/advertisement)

   a. _____

   b. _____

6. "The President called us. He wants us to visit him in the White House." (can, must/joke)

   a. _____

   b. _____

7. "Kim cooked a three-course meal by herself. Her mother didn't help." (can, must/help)

   a. _____

   b. _____

8. "Lee completed the race in under an hour." (could, might/an hour and a half)

   a. _____

   b. _____

6) Expressing Advice and Obligations About the Past

Read this story and write your advice about what went wrong in this bank robbery. Use *should have, shouldn't have,* or *ought to have.*

Several employees of a large factory decided to rob a bank a few blocks from the factory. The group thought the police would never look for them at the factory, so they went back to work after committing the crime. One problem: They had forgotten to remove their identification badges during the robbery.

1. They shouldn't have robbed a bank so close to their job.

2. _____

3. _____

4. _____

7) Expressing Regrets About the Past

Read the lists that describe Mr. O'Connor's regrets about the past—both the things that he did and the things that he didn't do. Complete the statements Mr. O'Connor would make about his regrets. Use *should have* or *shouldn't have* and phrases from the chart.

Things He Did	Things He Didn't Do
get married so young	exercise more
work so hard	take better care of his teeth
skip his medical checkups	learn to control his temper
live in the same town all his life	go to college

1. I shouldn't have lived in the same town all my life , but I didn't want to move.

2. _____ , but your grandmother and I fell madly in love.

3. _____ , but I hated going to the dentist.

4. _____ , but I never liked studying that much.

5. _____ , but I was too lazy to go to a gym.

6. _____ , but I had to earn enough money for my family.

7. _____ , but it's difficult to control.

8. _____ , but I was scared of doctors when I was younger.

COMBINING FORM, MEANING, AND USE

Choose two possible responses to complete each conversation.

1. **Jake:** I ought to have heard from my brother by now.

   Peter: _____
   a. What did he say?
   b. What time was he supposed to call? ⓑ
   c. Has he called you yet?
   d. He might have forgotten. ⓓ

2. **Ana:** Mmm. Something smells good.

   Rosa: _____
   a. Dad must have cooked dinner.
   b. Grandma should have made cookies.
   c. My sister must bake a cake for her cooking class.
   d. Mom may have fixed her famous spaghetti.

3. **Carlos:** Could Peter have come by while we were out?

   Gary: _____
   a. Yes, I guess he could.
   b. Yes, he might have.
   c. Yes, he may have been.
   d. No, he couldn't have.

4. **Tomek:** Weren't you supposed to start your new job last Monday?

   Teresa: _____
   a. No. I didn't have to start until Wednesday.
   b. Yes. I must have started on Monday.
   c. No. I shouldn't have started on Monday.
   d. Yes. And I did.

5. **Kedra:** It's Bill's birthday. Should I have gotten him something?

   Marcus: _____
   a. No, you must not have.
   b. No, you didn't have to.
   c. Yes, I think you were supposed to.
   d. Yes, you have to have.

6. **Soo-jin:** Wasn't Professor Chapman coming to the class party?

   Sun-hee: _____
   a. Should he have gone to a meeting?
   b. He should have forgotten about it.
   c. Could he have gotten too busy?
   d. He might have changed his mind.

7. **Celia:** We should have had dinner while we were downtown.

   Luisa: _____
   a. So you must not be hungry.
   b. I could have taken you to a nice restaurant on Main Street.
   c. Why were we supposed to have dinner downtown?
   d. You're right. I'm sorry that we didn't.

8. **Satomi:** Kim moved to San Francisco last month.

   Takeshi: _____ I saw her less than a week ago.
   a. She can't have moved.
   b. She ought not to have moved.
   c. She should have moved.
   d. She couldn't have.

Read the letter that Miguel wrote to Gina, an advice columnist, and complete the task below.

Dear Gina
by
Gina Burke

I have a problem with my wife, Marta. She is jealous of my old girlfriend, Diane. Diane and I dated in college. I used to think about marrying her, but I waited too long to ask (I think I was too shy), and she married someone else. After Marta and I got married, Diane got divorced. Well, soon after, Diane and I had lunch together a few times. I didn't think Marta would approve, even though Diane and I are just friends, so I told her I was with my friend Steve. Marta found out the truth and told me to stop seeing Diane. Well, I have promised not to see Diane anymore, but I would like to know what I should have done. Was I wrong to see her? Should I have told my wife? What could I have done differently? I feel pretty confused right now.

—*Miguel G.*
San Jose, CA

Imagine that you have received this letter while Gina is on vacation and you must write an answer for Gina. On a separate sheet of paper, write a one-paragraph answer to Miguel. Tell him what he should or shouldn't have done or how he could have done things differently. Use *might have*, *could have*, *should have*, and *shouldn't have* when possible.

> Boy, Miguel, you are confused. I think you're the problem
> here, not your wife. First of all, you shouldn't have lied to
> her about seeing Diane . . . .

Chapters 7–8

A. Rewrite these sentences, choosing from the modals in the box. Do not change the meaning. Use each modal only once and change the form as necessary.

can't	ought to
could	has got to
might	shouldn't
may not be	should

1. I heard on Channel 7 that we might have a severe storm tonight.

   _____

2. You could have grown taller if you had eaten your spinach at every meal.

   _____

3. It must be very difficult for you to see your friend sick.

   _____

4. He ought to have been here an hour ago.

   _____

5. I'm fairly certain this won't take more than about five minutes.

   _____

6. That rumor about Rick couldn't possibly be true!

   _____

7. We really should call Paulo tonight.

   _____

8. Maybe she isn't coming to class today.

   _____

B. Read each situation. Then rewrite the sentences, using modals to express the meaning in parentheses. There may be more than one correct answer.

> Hiro has been working overtime a lot lately.

9. He needs the money. (possibility)

_____

10. He's saving for a new car. (conclusion)

_____

11. Hiro's boss is grateful. (obligation)

_____

12. Hiro is exhausted. (understanding)

_____

> I was calling Teresa for hours last night, but the line was busy.

13. She took the phone off the hook. (past possibility)

_____

14. She was talking to her boyfriend. (logical conclusion about the past)

_____

15. Her phone is out of order. (guess)

_____

16. She wasn't on the phone that long. (disbelief about the past)

_____

> Kate just got her driver's license.

17. She isn't old enough to drive. (disbelief)

_____

18. She had a birthday recently. (guess about the past)

_____

19. She drives carefully. (advice)

_____

C. Circle **all** the possible words or phrases to complete each sentence.

20. Kate is getting married next month. She _____ very excited.

    a. could be
    b. must be
    c. might be
    d. can be

21. Bill went home early today. He _____ well.

    a. must not have felt
    b. must not be feeling
    c. mustn't feel
    d. must not feel

22. Paul is not answering the phone. He _____ away.

    a. should be
    b. must be
    c. can't be
    d. might be

23. Nancy isn't here yet. _____ she have gotten stuck in traffic?

    a. Should
    b. Ought to
    c. Must
    d. Could

24. Should Mr. Ponce have been at the meeting this morning? Yes, _____ .

    a. he could have
    b. he should have
    c. he should have been
    d. he could

25. The police have very little doubt: The Bayside Burglar _____ guilty of the crime.

    a. has to be
    b. must be
    c. might be
    d. can be

26. The students in Mrs. Costa's class must stand up when they want to speak, but we _____ stand in our class. We're allowed to stay seated.

    a. may not
    b. mustn't
    c. don't have to
    d. can't

27. There's a story in the paper about a man who says he was kidnapped by tiny gray men with huge eyes. The man _____ .

    a. should see a doctor
    b. must be crazy
    c. is probably lying
    d. has got to have a vivid imagination

28. Chris had his cellular phone, so he _____ us. Why didn't he?

    a. could call
    b. might have called
    c. should be calling
    d. could have called

29. I'm tired of that song. I _____ it twenty times already on the radio today.

    a. might be hearing
    b. 've got to have heard
    c. have to hear
    d. must have heard

30. What do I think of the story? Well, it sounds pretty silly, but I guess it _____ true.

    a. can be
    b. could be
    c. might be
    d. should be

Answer Key

Chapter 1 The Present

Exercise 1 (p. 1)

1. line 4:   eats
   line 5:   runs out
   line 10: goes
   line 16: knows
   line 17: takes
   line 21: studies
   line 21: takes
   line 22: hires
   line 23: leaves
   line 25: does . . . want
   line 27: knows
   line 29: don't get
   line 31: work
   line 32: come
   line 37: realize
   line 41: changes

2. line 11: 's getting
   line 34: are becoming
   line 37: are spending
   line 39: (are) playing
   line 40: (are) sleeping

3. line 23:   She never leaves them in the hands of a babysitter even if she does sometimes want to have an afternoon for herself.
   b

Exercise 2 (p. 2)

2. Does his sister Fumie study in sixth grade?
3. How many days does she go to juku?
4. Does their mother study with her children?
5. Does she teach them herself?
6. Why don't Japanese fathers get involved in their children's education?
7. When do they usually come home?
8. What do more Japanese realize today?

Exercise 3 (p. 3)

2. are filling up
3. 're looking
4. 're walking
5. 's . . . doing
6. Is . . . arguing
7. isn't arguing
8. 's . . . wishing
9. are taking off
10. is . . . getting started
11. is taking
12. is doing
13. is making
14. are raising
15. is starting

Exercise 4 (p. 4)

2. PC
3. PC
4. SP
5. SP
6. SP

2.
b. 1
c. 6
d. 3
e. 4
f. 2

Exercise 5 (p. 5)

2. A   6. S
3. S   7. S
4. A   8. S
5. A

Exercise 6 (p. 5)

2. b   3. a   4. b   5. c   6. c   7. b   8. a

Exercise 7 (p. 7)

'm writing
I ~~write~~ this letter because I have a serious problem. I
I don't believe
work in a stressful job, but ~~I'm not believing~~ it's worse

than what most people face at work. My problem is that
I cry   go   know
~~I'm crying~~ too easily when things ~~goes~~ wrong. I ~~knowing~~ I

have to get stronger. I don't deal well with

disappointment or criticism. ~~It's being~~ very embarrassing.
is becoming
In fact, the situation ~~becomes~~ more and more difficult.

What advice do you have for me?

Cry Baby in Dallas

Dear Cry Baby:
get
   Most of us ~~gets~~ upset when others criticize us. But
You don't appear
you are ~~being~~ right: ~~You're not appearing~~ professional

when you cry at work. Sometimes we ~~needs~~ to cry, but

tears don't ~~belongs~~ on the job. If you think you're going

to cry, go to the restroom and do it there. And please, see

a therapist to help you with your emotions.

Exercise 8 (p. 7)

Answers will vary.

Chapter 2 The Past

Exercise 1 (p. 8)

1. line 2: traveled   line 11: opposed, hoped
   line 3: met   line 12: threatened
   line 5: expressed   line 13: approached
   line 7: returned   line 14: earned
   line 9: began   line 17: made
2. line 9: was becoming
   line 10: were killing
   line 15: was sleeping
3. line 9: . . . when Fossey began her research
   line 15: . . . while she was sleeping at her campsite

Exercise 2 (p. 9)

Conversation 1

Hector: I overslept. I didn't wake up until 8:30.

  Rosa: Did your boss see you?

Hector: She saw me when I came in.

  Rosa: Did she say anything to you?

Hector: She didn't say anything, but she gave me a dirty look.

Conversation 2

  Eva: Sorry. Were you trying to sleep?

Elena: No. I wasn't sleeping. I was reading.

  Eva: Well, first Sasha and I were watching a great TV program.

Elena: Is that why you were laughing so hard?

  Eva: For part of the time. Later, we were laughing because we were looking at some old pictures of you!

Exercise 3 (p. 10)

A. 2. when you ate in that fancy restaurant?
   3. after I gave you my number?
   4. when you were growing up?
   5. before you had a car?
   6. while you were unemployed?

B. b. 3   c. 2   d. 6   e. 1   f. 5

C. a. 4, 6   b. 2, 3, 5

Exercise 4 (p. 11)

2. were waiting for   11. was shaking
3. heard   12. introducing
4. looked   13. chatted
5. didn't see   14. were talking
6. knew   15. realized
7. saw   16. was getting
8. was standing   17. said
9. was washing
10. called

Exercise 5 (p. 11)

A. 2. a   3. a   4. b   5. b   6. b
B. 2. c   3. a, b, c   4. a, b   5. c, e   6. a, b

Exercise 6 (p. 12)

2. b, c   3. a, b   4. c   5. b   6. a, c

Exercise 7 (p. 13)

~~I'm having~~ *I have* so many wonderful memories of my childhood. ~~While~~ *When* I was three years old, my family moved to Costa Rica. For the first few years, we lived in a small apartment. Then, when ~~it's~~ *it was* time for my brother and me to start school, my parents ~~were buying~~ *bought* our first house. For the first time, I had my own room and didn't ~~had~~ *have* to share with my sister. I ~~was loving~~ *loved* that room! My mother ~~was liking~~ *liked* to sew, and she made a beautiful bedspread and matching curtains.

We didn't have a lot of free time during the week, but weekends were always ~~being~~ a lot of fun. On Saturdays, we always ~~play~~ *played* games together. Sunday was my favorite day because we almost always went to the beach. We ~~were packing~~ *packed* a big lunch, and Dad barbecue*d* hamburgers or chicken. We kids were ~~being~~ sleepy after we ~~were eating~~ *ate*, so we spread blankets under a big tree and ~~take~~ *took* naps.

Exercise 8 (p. 14)

Answers will vary.

Chapter 3 Future Forms

Exercise 1 (p. 15)

1. line 5: are going to be   line 31: will understand
   line 8: will be growing   line 32: will invent
   line 10: (will be) transplanting   line 34: will talk
   line 14: will get   line 40: will be
   line 15: won't be traveling   line 41: will be
   line 21: will be   line 44: will die
   line 24: 'll be flying   line 46: will . . . be like
   line 26: will come   line 49: is going out of business
   line 27: (will) pick . . . up   line 53: 'll be doing
2. line 43: When that happens . . .
3. b

Exercise 2 (p. 16)

2. Jane will be teaching her nieces how to bowl.
3. David will be shopping with his grandmother.
4. Takeshi will be helping Jessica.
5. Celia will be catching up on her homework.
6. Rachel will be working.

Exercise 3 (p. 16)

2. It begins
3. When does it end?
4. It ends
5. When do the boat races start?
6. They start
7. How long do they/the boat races last?
8. They last
9. How much does the celebration cost?
10. It costs

Exercise 4 (p. 17)

2. b, c   3. b   4. a, b, c   5. a   6. a, b, c

Exercise 5 (p. 17)

2. Before she goes food shopping, she's going to write down the grocery list./She's going to write down the grocery list before she goes food shopping.
3. After she bakes the turkey for six hours at 375°, she's going to take it out of the oven./She's going to take the turkey out of the oven after she bakes it for six hours at 375°.
4. As soon as she polishes the silver, she's going to set the table./She's going to set the table as soon as she polishes the silver.
5. She's going to wait to add the dressing until she prepares all the ingredients for the salad./Until she prepares all the ingredients for the salad, she's going to wait to add the dressing.
6. She's going to wash the kitchen floor after she sweeps it./After she sweeps the kitchen floor, she's going to wash it.

Exercise 6 (p. 18)

(Any combination of the following forms is acceptable.)

b. **Hiro:** What are you going to do next Saturday?
   Koji: Yuko and I are spending the day at the beach.

2. a. **Ben:** When are you going to finish final exams?
   Kevin: I'm finishing next week.
   b. **Ben:** When are you finishing final exams?
   Kevin: I'm going to finish next week.

3. a. **David:** How are you celebrating your birthday this year?
   Kate: My parents are going to throw me a big party.
   b. **David:** How are you going to celebrate your birthday this year?
   Kate: My parents are throwing me a big party.

4. a. **Emily:** What are you going to do after graduation?
   Tony: I'm leaving on a trip to Mexico.
   b. **Emily:** What are you doing after graduation?
   Tony: I'm going to leave on a trip to Mexico.

Exercise 7 (p. 19)

People predict that genetic engineering *will have* ~~has~~ a major effect on our food supply in the future. Genetically engineered fruits, vegetables, and animals will help increase the food supply. For example, it is possible that people *will grow* ~~are growing~~ tropical fruits such as bananas, coconuts, and pineapples in colder climates such as Canada or Russia. Foods on supermarket shelves are going *to* taste better and last longer. Since these foods won't spoil as quickly, they *will be* ~~are being~~ abundant and cheap.

These new foods *are* also going to be better for you. Scientists *will* manipulate the DNA of many foods to make them more nutritious and allergy-free. Potatoes *will have* ~~will be having~~ a special gene so that when people make French fries, they *won't soak* ~~aren't soaking~~ up as much oil. And there may even be special fruits and vegetables that act like vaccines. So instead of getting a shot to prevent disease, people *will eat* ~~are eating~~ an apple or a carrot!

Exercise 8 (p. 19)

Answers will vary.

See page 71 for Key to Review: Chapter 1-3.

Chapter 4 The Present Perfect

Exercise 1 (p. 22)

1. line 12: have gone
   line 16: has maintained
   line 17: have returned
   line 21: have performed
   line 23: has succeeded
   line 27: have found

Exercise 2 (p. 23)

2. 've been
3. has been
4. have you ordered
5. has come
6. haven't ordered
7. haven't eaten
8. Have you seen
9. 've eaten
10. 've never had
11. 've paid

12. 've had
13. 've raised
14. Have you decided
15. Have you heard
16. has prepared

Exercise 3 (p. 24)

A. 2. Eighty-nine percent have told a white lie.
3. Sixty-seven percent have called in sick to work when they were healthy.
4. Sixty percent have parked illegally.
5. Fifty-seven percent have cheated on an exam.
6. Forty-three percent have written a personal E-mail at work.
7. Thirty-eight percent have made a long-distance phone call at work.
8. Nineteen percent have cut into a line.

B. 2. Q: Have you ever told a white lie?
   A: (Answers will vary.)
3. Q: Have you ever called in sick to work when you were healthy?
   A: (Answers will vary.)
4. Q: Have you ever parked illegally?
   A: (Answers will vary.)
5. Q: Have you ever cheated on an exam?
   A: (Answers will vary.)
6. Q: Have you ever written a personal e-mail at work?
   A: (Answers will vary.)
7. Q: Have you ever made a long-distance phone call at work?
   A: (Answers will vary.)
8. Q: Have you ever cut into a line?
   A: (Answers will vary.)

Exercise 4 (p. 25)

2. since
3. recently/lately
4. lately/recently
5. just
6. for
7. since
8. for

Exercise 5 (p. 26)

2. Gina: Have you chosen a hotel in Buenos Aires yet?
   Steve: Yes, I chose the Olympic.
3. Gina: Have you paid the room deposit yet?
   Steve: No, I haven't. I will tomorrow.
4. Steve: Have you renewed our passports?
   Gina: Yes, I have. I did it on Wednesday.
5. Steve: Have you reserved a rental car?
   Gina: No, I haven't. I've been too busy.

Exercise 6 (p. 27)

2. b   3. a   4. a   5. a   6. b   7. b   8. a   9. a   10. a

Exercise 7 (p. 28)

Answers will vary.

Chapter 5 The Present Perfect Continuous

Exercise 1 (p. 29)

1. line 3: has . . . been working on
   line 6: 's been working
   line 8: has been making
   line 16: has been frightening

2. line 3: has . . . been working on
   line 6: 's been working
   line 8: has been making
   line 16: has been frightening

Exercise 2 (p. 30)

Conversation 1
2. 've been calling
3. has been trying
4. 've been asking

Conversation 2
1. Has she been avoiding
2. 's been working
3. 's been getting
4. hasn't been doing
5. 's been taking

Conversation 3
1. have you been planning
2. 've been preparing
3. have been making
4. 've been watching
5. 've been improving
6. 've been skating

Exercise 3 (p. 31)

2. He's been going to parties lately, and he hasn't been studying enough.
3. He's just been talking to his grandmother, and she hasn't been feeling well.
4. She hasn't been sleeping well lately because she's been having nightmares.
5. They haven't been spending time with friends recently because they've been painting their house.
6. She hasn't been going straight home after work because she's been going to the hospital to visit her uncle.

Exercise 4 (p. 32)

2. a   3. a   4. a   5. b   6. a   7. b   8. a

Exercise 5 (p. 32)

Conversation 1
2. 've been thinking
3. haven't spoken
4. called
5. 's been traveling
6. (has) promised

Conversation 2
1. Have you read
2. haven't seen
3. has been making
4 knew
5. 's worked
6. haven't seen
7. Has she been working
8. 's been taking
9. loved

Exercise 6 (p. 33)

2. b, c   5. a, c
3. a, b   6. a, c
4. c, d

Exercise 7 (p. 34)

Soccer is the most popular international team sport. Historians believe that people ~~has~~ *have* been playing soccer since the year 217 A.D., when the first game ~~has been~~ *was* part of a victory celebration in England. Soccer became popular in Europe over the centuries, and eventually it spread throughout most of the world. In the United States, soccer has always been ~~being~~ secondary to American football. Recently, however, soccer has *been* ∧ growing in popularity.

In 1904, several nations ~~have~~ formed the International Federation of Football (FIFA), which has been regulating international competition ~~since~~ *for* over a century. Since 1930, the World Cup ~~have~~ *has* been bringing countries together. And although women ~~weren't~~ *haven't been* playing soccer for as long as men have, an important international event, the Women's World Cup, has been ~~taken~~ *taking* place every four years since 1991.

Exercise 8 (p. 35)

Answers will vary.

Chapter 6 The Past Perfect and the Past Perfect Continuous

Exercise 1 (p. 36)

1. line 2:   had been thinking
   line 10: had been going
2. line 3: 'd . . . had   line 11: had offered
   line 4: hadn't been   line 12: hadn't . . . discussed
   line 5: had known   line 14: had . . . wanted
   line 6: had . . . argued   line 16: had . . . known
   line 6: had become   line 17: had . . . loved
3. *a* is incorrect. The past perfect uses only one auxiliary.

   b and *c* are correct.

Exercise 2 (p. 37)

2. he had never washed his own dishes.
3. he had never made his own bed.
4. he had never done his own laundry.

Exercise 3 (p. 37)

2. When Chris and Emily arrived, the group had been pulling weeds for twenty-five minutes.
3. When Sasha came, the group had been washing the benches for five minutes.
4. When Jane got there, the group had been painting the benches for half an hour thirty minutes.
5. When Mr. and Mrs. Rivera came, the group had been cleaning the playground for twenty minutes.
6. When Rick arrived, the group had been raking leaves for fifteen minutes.

Exercise 4 (p. 38)

2. Picasso had drawn his first picture before he spoke his first word. OR Before he spoke his first word, Picasso had drawn his first picture.
3. Picasso had lived in Málaga until he entered the Royal Academy in Madrid. OR Until he entered the Royal Academy in Madrid, Picasso had lived in Málaga.
4. Picasso had produced more than 1,000 works of art by the time he was 23 years old. OR By the time he was 23 years old, Picasso had produced more than 1,000 works of art.
5. Picasso became well-known after he had moved to Paris. OR After Picasso had moved to Paris, he became well-known.
6. The history of art changed forever after Picasso painted *Les Demoisels d' Avignon*. OR After Picasso painted *Les Demoisels d' Avignon*, the history of art changed forever.
7. Picasso painted his anti-war painting *Guernica* after the Nazis bombed Guernica, Spain. OR After the Nazis bombed Guernica, Spain, Picasso painted his anti-war painting *Guernica*.
8. Picasso had lived in Paris for many years when he moved to southern France. OR When he moved to southern France, Picasso had lived in Paris for many years.
9. Jacqueline Roque had been Picasso's companion for seven years before they got married. OR Before they got married, Jacqueline Roque had been Picasso's companion for seven years.
10. Picasso had lived in Mougins for almost 20 years before he died. OR Before he died, Picasso had lived in Mougins for almost 20 years.

Exercise 5 (p. 40)

B. 2. The group hadn't cut the grass yet, but they had already pulled weeds.
3. The group hadn't raked leaves yet, but they had already picked up the trash.
4. The group hadn't planted flowers yet, but they had already trimmed the trees.
5. The group hadn't emptied the trash cans yet, but they had planted flowers.

Exercise 6 (p. 41)

2. I bought a new car because my old one had been acting up.
3. My eyes were aching although I'd taken a nap after lunch.
4. My eyes were aching because I'd been studying very hard.
5. My eyes were aching because I'd been working at the computer for hours.
6. My eyes were aching because I'd left my glasses at home.
7. My teacher loved my report although I hadn't worked very hard on it.
8. My grades were terrible although I'd been studying very hard.
9. My grades were terrible because I hadn't been taking good class notes lately.
10. I'd never bought a new car although my parents had always promised to help with the payments.
11. I'd never bought a new car because I'd never had enough money.
12. I got a low grade on my report because I hadn't worked very hard on it.

Exercise 7 (p. 42)

2. b, d   4. b, d   6. b, c
3. b, c   5. a, c

Exercise 8 (p. 42)

Answers will vary.

See page 71 for Key to Review: Chapters 4-6.

Chapter 7 Modals of Possibility

Exercise 1 (p. 46)

1. line 4: could   line 12: could
   line 5: 's got to   line 13: should
   line 9: could   line 15: may not
   line 11: might   line 16: ought to
2. a, c

Exercise 2 (p. 47)

2. Correct
3. Incorrect
   I *may not* be in class tomorrow.
4. Correct
5. Incorrect
   Could the accused man be innocent?
6. Incorrect
   This *can't* be right. It makes no sense.
7. Correct
8. Incorrect
   Steve must feel terrible about this.

Exercise 3 (p. 47)

Conversation 1

2. ought to be
3. he can't be
4. may be
5. we might miss
6. That has to be
7. could he be calling
8. He must be calling

Conversation 2

1. This can't be happening
2. we might be running out of
3. How could that be
4. has to be
5. could be
6. we should be
7. ought to be

Exercise 4 (p. 48)

a. 2, 3, 5
b. 1, 10
c. 4, 8, 9
d. 6, 7

Exercise 5 (p. 49)

2. should/ought to
3. could/might/may
4. must/'ve got to/have to
5. must/have got to/have to
6. should/ought to
7. should/ought to
8. should/must/'s got to/has to/
9. should/ought to/must
10. could/might/may

Exercise 6 (p. 50)

2. It should be/ought to be cooler tonight.
3. It could/may/might rain tomorrow.
4. It could/may/might be warmer on Thursday.
5. It won't snow on Saturday.
6. The temperature will drop tomorrow.

Exercise 7 (p. 50)

2. D
   She's got to be upset.
3. D
   I might be late tonight.
4. S
5. D
   It might/may rain any minute.
6. S
7. S

8. D

It ought to be great.

9. D

This must/has got to be the place.

10. S

Exercise 8 (p. 52)

Hi, Dr. Carter. I'm writing to tell you that I probably *won't* ~~mightn't~~ be in class next week. My grandfather may

needs̶ an operation, and my parents want me to come

home to be with the family. No one has told me yet what

kind of surgery Grandpa needs, but it *must/has to/has got to* ~~should~~ be serious.

Otherwise, my family wouldn't be suggesting that I make

the long trip home. *You* ~~You'll~~ may find this a bit unusual, but

I'm very close to my grandfather. I know this absence

could t̶o̶ put my grade in danger, but I'll work very hard

so that I don't fall behind.

may not You ~~mayn't~~ be very happy about this, but I need to

ask a special favor. Do you think you might *be* ~~being~~ able to

E-mail me next week's assignments? That way, I *may be* ~~maybe~~

able to do some of them while I'm away. I'm not sure, but *be* I should ~~am~~ getting back to Los Angeles by April 1.

Thank you very much.

Matt Kennedy

Exercise 9 (p. 52)

Answers will vary.

Chapter 8 Past Modals

Exercise 1 (p. 53)

1. line 7: couldn't have been
   line 9: may have been
   line 10: couldn't have used
   line 12: must have provided
   line 14: could have pulled
   line 14: would have worn down
   line 15: would have . . . polished

2. a, b

Exercise 2 (p. 54)

2. I could have picked you up at the airport last weekend.

3. The students might not have understood everything on yesterday's test.

4. David must have been at the office yesterday afternoon.

5. We could have gone to the mountains last summer.

6. There must have been a lot of traffic this morning.

7. The company might have solved its financial problems last year.

8. You shouldn't have stayed up late last night.

Exercise 3 (p. 54)

Conversation 1

2. could have happened
3. might not have received
4. must have gone

Conversation 2

1. might have caught
2. should have gotten
3. shouldn't have taken
4. had to have been laughing

Exercise 4 (p. 55)

1. b. She might have/may have/could have secretly returned to the United States.

   c. She must have/had to have/'s got to have run out of fuel and crashed.

2. a. The builders must have/had to have/have got to have traveled over land and sea to bring the stones for the monument.

   b. The building of the monument couldn't have/can't have started before 3000 B.C.

   c. The structure might have/could have/may have been a temple.

Exercise 5 (p. 56)

2. They couldn't have finished the homework. They may have started the homework.

3. They can't have gotten to Washington in less than an hour. They might have gotten there in less than three hours.

4. Rick couldn't have robbed the bank. Someone else must have robbed the bank.

5. They can't have won a million dollars. They must have received an advertisement.

6. The President can't have called you yesterday. It must have been a joke.

7. Kim can't have cooked a three-course meal by herself. Her mother must have helped.

8. Lee couldn't have completed the race in under an hour. He might have completed it in an hour and a half.

Exercise 6 (p. 57)

Answers will vary. Some examples are:

2. They should have/ought to have removed their identification badges during the robbery.
3. They shouldn't have/ought not to have gone back to work after committing the crime.
4. They should have realized the police would find them.

Exercise 7 (p. 57)

2. I shouldn't have/ought not to have gotten married so young
3. I should have/ought to have taken better care of my teeth
4. I should have/ought to have gone to college
5. I should have/ought to have exercised more

6. I shouldn't have/ought not to have worked so hard
7. I should have/ought to have learned to control my temper
8. I shouldn't have/ought not to have skipped my medical checkups.

Exercise 8 (p. 58)

2. a, d   4. a, d   6. c, d   8. a, d
3. b, d   5. b, c   7. b, d

Exercise 9 (p. 59)

Answers will vary.

See page 71 for Key to Review Chapters 7-8.

Key to Chapter Reviews

Review: Chapters 1–3

A.
1. c
2. b
3. c
4. a
5. a
6. c
7. a
8. b
9. b
10. c
11. c
12. b
13. c
14. a

B.
15. How ~~was~~ *did* the fire ~~starting~~ *start*?
16. The children ~~played~~ *were playing* in the yard when it started to rain.
17. The movie is about a group of teenagers who ~~are getting~~ *get* lost in the forest.
18. I know these jeans ~~are looking~~ *look* terrible, but all my other pants are in the laundry.
19. When Kedra was a child, she ~~would have~~ *had* a lot of friends.
20. Marcus and I won't be getting ~~marry~~ *married* next year because we just broke off our engagement.
21. The Chiefs will be the champions this year because they're definitely ~~winning~~ *going to win* tomorrow night's game.
22. I promise that I will ~~be finishing~~ *finish* my homework.
23. If you have time, will you ~~be stopping~~ *stop* and pick up some bread on your way home?
24. Carlos is usually ~~being~~ very level-headed, but today he's overreacting to everything.
25. I was jogging in the park ~~while~~ *when* I fell and hurt my left ankle.

C.
26. b, c   27. b, c   28. a, b   29. b, d   30. a, d

Review: Chapters 4–6

A.
1. How long have the police been trying to solve that crime?
2. How long had the police been trying to solve that crime?
3. X
4. How long did the police try to solve that crime?
5. 2, 4
6. We'd shopped at that store for years.
7. We shopped at the store for years.
8. We've been shopping at that store for years.
9. 6, 7
10. They've had that car since 1998.
11. They'd had that car since 1998.
12. X
13. X
14. X
15. 10

B.
16. e
17. c
18. d
19. g
20. b
21. f
22. a

C.
23. X
Jenny **had** been walking for hours when she noticed it was late.
24. ✓
25. X
Yuji **has** been cooking all day for the party.
26. X
Until we went to France last year, **we'd** never eaten snails.
27. ✓
28. X
Alex won the perfect-attendance award because he **hadn't missed** a day since school started.
29. X
The American Revolutionary War **lasted** from 1775 to 1783.
30. ✓

Review: Chapters 7–8

A.
1. I heard on Channel 7 that we could have a severe storm tonight.
2. You might have grown taller if you had eaten your spinach at every meal.
3. It has got to be very difficult for you to see your friend sick.
4. He should have been here an hour ago.
5. I'm fairly certain this shouldn't take more than about five minutes.
6. That rumor about Rick can't possibly be true!
7. We really ought to call Paulo tonight.
8. She may not be coming to class today.

B.
9. He may need the money./He might need the money./He could need the money.
10. He must be saving for a car./He has to be saving for a car./He's got to be saving for a car.
11. Hiro's boss should be grateful./Hiro's boss ought to be grateful.
12. Hiro must be exhausted./Hiro had to be exhausted./Hiro has got to be exhausted.

13. She could have taken the phone off the hook./
    She might have taken the phone off the hook./
    She may have taken the phone off the hook.
14. She must have been talking to her boyfriend./
    She had to have been talking to her boyfriend./
    She has to have been talking to her boyfriend./
    She's got to have been talking to her boyfriend.
15. Her phone could be out of order./Her phone
    might be out of order./Her phone may be out of
    order.
16. She couldn't have been on the phone that long!/
    She can't have been on the phone that long!

17. She couldn't be old enough to drive!/She can't
    be old enough to drive!
18. She must have had a birthday recently./She
    might have had a birthday recently.
19. She should drive carefully.

C.
20. b	**26.** c
21. a, b, d	**27.** a, b, c, d
22. b, d	**28.** d
23. d	**29.** b, d
24. b, c	**30.** b, c
25. a, b	